The Christian Parent's T

Print-Facsimile Pocket Booklet

The Christian Parent's Toolkit

By Sarah Johnson

continuum

Published by Continuum
The Tower Building, 11 York Road, London SE1 7NX
80 Maiden Lane, Suite 704, New York, NY 10038

www.continuumbooks.com

First published 2008

British Library Cataloguing-in-Publication Data
A catalogue record for this book is available from the British Library.

ISBN-13 978-08264-9784-0 (paperback)
ISBN-10 0-8264-9784-5 (paperback)

Typeset by YHT Ltd, London
Printed and bound in Great Britain by
Cromwell Press Ltd., Trowbridge, Wiltshire

Contents

Introduction 1

My dear friends, let us love each other, since love is from God
and everyone who lives is a child of God and knows God.[1]

1 John 4.7

There are thousands of parents up and down the UK who belong
to Christian denominations or have connections with one. Many
of these are young, hopeful and thoughtful people, who feel
unease at the idea of a purely materialistic world without spirituality, which the secularization of the West entails. Many of these
parents are touched by the beauty of the story of Jesus Christ and
are prepared to give religion a chance; these are perhaps young
parents who feel uncomfortable when they read yet another dia-
tribe against God, yet another attack on Christians who are given
little chance to defend themselves.

There are thousands of parents, in short, who would quite like
there to be a God of the kind Jesus promised, and would like to tell
their children that there is such a God, but do not know where to
find the evidence for Him.

These parents probably also are well aware of the saying 'it takes
a village to raise a child', and want their children to grow up with a
sense of community. But they are also aware that a 'gated community' patrolled by security guards is not the same thing as a
village. There are thousands of parents who are tentatively wondering if they would fit in at their local church . . . but are not sure
whether they would find anyone there like themselves, are not
sure where to start, are not sure if it will be worth it.

For these parents I have put together a toolkit. The toolkit is not
the same as an armoury. The tools found inside it are not intended
to be used as weapons against your children, but as tools for
shaping their lives. They include tools for building opportunities
for spiritual growth, for contact with the eternal and for

developing a deeper relationship with God. They include tools for adding strength to the walls of your life. They are to be used to create, shape and construct. Some of them are imaginary tools – they are symbols of parental virtues – whereas one or two are perfectly real (such as Wellington boots and an alarm clock).

I want to show in this book how the Christian faith is a support for parents and families and not some kind of antique hindrance. I want to show you different ways in which this faith can help you find a path through the thorny thickets of parenting and family life.

Often, in the course of compiling this book, I have met up with families that are intensely grateful for the structure they belong to – their religion. This faith, which is routinely mocked by comedians, despised by the media and dismissed as superstition by academics, is, quite simply, their rock. It is their solid ground, their lighthouse, their lodestar. It provides not only comfort but also community and rhythm. It provides an unmoving star to steer by. It provides a firm surface from which to launch out and a soft surface on which to land.

When followed humbly and with love, this faith does not smother thought, but encourages it. It does not crush creativity but inspires it. It does not close doors, but opens them. This faith guides the young and the old – but as well as offering answers, it fills their heads with interesting questions, and often subverts smug or lazy assumptions. It channels and nurtures the human search for truth beyond the merely seen.

You can dip into the toolkit whenever you have something you want to fix, or else you can open it up and spread its contents out on the ground for major projects. You may not need all the tools at the same time but you will certainly need them all in the long run.

Note

1. All biblical quotations are from the New Jerusalem Bible, standard edition.

A road map

2

Imagine no religion.

John Lennon

That Jones shall worship the god within him turns out ultimately to mean that Jones shall worship Jones.

G. K. Chesterton

Part of me ... thinks I'm God Almighty.

John Lennon

If something terrible happens to you – something gut-wrenchingly
awful, which leaves your life in tatters – who will comfort you?
Who will put their hands on your shoulders and steady their
trembling? Who will make sure you have a cup of tea and a place
to sit and weep? Who will stick around to see that you get enough
rest and food; that you remember to have a shower and change
your clothes? Who will listen to your sorrow?

Will you be comforted by members of your family? If so, you
are lucky indeed – but what if the family themselves are the cause
of your pain? What if you are one of the many people with no
close family?

Do you have friends to turn to? If you do, what if they blame
you for your disaster? What if your tragedy, whatever it is, casts a
shadow over your presence; splits some of them into 'pro' and
'anti' camps, and makes deserters of the rest?

These sombre questions crop up in all of our minds at one time
or other but mostly when we are setting out on some new
undertaking. Parenthood is an unknown territory full of hazards,
and when setting out on any hazardous journey we are always
advised to know who to call in an emergency. Those who fall by
the wayside most rapidly are those with no support structure; those

who find the road hardest do not have a family, or friends, or a community, or any sense of true belonging on which they can lay claim.

Setting out on a hazardous journey is also made easier with the help of a map. Maps are made by people who have travelled that road before. They have found out where the dangers are and have worked out ways of avoiding them. These people are in the past, a long line of them stretching out behind us for hundreds of years, linked to us by tradition. When we discard tradition we may sometimes be discarding some good advice: when presented with a road map, we are well advised to read it carefully and we generally assume that it has been made by people who've checked the route out before us. They may not have got it all down accurately, there may be mistakes on the map, but most of us feel more secure with the map handy than without.

There is a growing tendency to set aside the role which a strong religious faith, and particularly the most common faith of all – Christianity (to which three out of every five adults in the UK claim to adhere[1]) – plays in all aspects of social welfare. Looking at the news coverage of Christianity and the general attitude to it in the broadcast and print media, you would suppose that Christianity, far from being the road map of morality, was such a minority interest as to rate as little more than an offbeat cult.

On the other hand, if I pick up one of the broadsheet daily newspapers I will find a whole section devoted to theatre and performance arts. This section of the newspaper merits its own staff and its own contingent of specialist correspondents. It will include several theatre reviews a week and, in addition, a healthy sprinkling of interviews and features throughout other sections of the paper. It is very entertaining and I love reading about the theatre, even though I only go to see a play perhaps four or five times a year. Even at that low level, I rate as a frequent theatregoer compared with most people: less than a quarter of the country's adult population (24 per cent) goes to the theatre even as often as once a year.[2]

A slightly larger number, more than a quarter (26 per cent) of the country's adult population, attends a church service at least once a year. More than half of the churchgoers in the country (7.6

million) attend at least once a month and a solid core of 4.9 million people 'do it' (as a bumper sticker would say) every week.

The theatregoers' frequency of 'doing it' is spread out in completely the opposite way: The vast majority of them only go to the theatre once a year as a special treat on a birthday or as a traditional trip to the panto at Christmas. A tiny, minuscule proportion go to a theatre as often as once a month, but hardly anyone other than theatre critics goes to the theatre once a week or more. In other words, the bulk of the churchgoers are regulars, while the bulk of the theatregoers are occasional visitors.

As a journalist I can well imagine the stunned and contemptuous reaction I would get if I were to suggest to any news or features editor of an upmarket broadsheet that, since theatregoing is such a minority interest, and organized Christianity evidently so much more popular, why not scrap the theatre reviews altogether and use the space for news and information about what goes on inside the rich and constantly surprising variety of churches? Why not employ a few more columnists and leader writers who believe in God, instead of dozens of metropolitan pundits who feel that part of their job is to attack religion, and Christianity in particular?

Well, if I made such a suggestion, I would barely have time to clear my desk before being ejected, possibly forcibly, from the building. Yet it is hard to fathom why. For one thing, the open hostility to Christianity which I perceive in the 'quality' media is clearly not based on the preferences of their target readership, listeners or viewers.

Surveys show that churchgoers tend to be middle class and therefore more likely also to do middle-class things – such as reading broadsheet newspapers and listening to Radio 4. Since they go to church, they presumably believe in God and seek to follow Christ: it is strange, then, that broadsheet editors seek to woo them with headlines such as 'Enough religion. Stop shoving it down my throat' (Carol Sarler, *The Times*, 13 September 2007) or 'Shout your doubt out loud, my fellow unbelievers' (Matthew Parris, *The Times*, 21 April 2007). Interviews with prominent atheist campaigners such as Richard Dawkins, Christopher Hitchens and A. C. Grayling are plentiful, respectful and adoring; interviews with prominent churchmen and churchwomen are few and far between.

The problem is that going to church is an activity associated (in the mind of the average newspaper editor, though without any strong evidence from demographic surveys) with older generations. Wrongly, it may also be associated in this putative editor's mind with lower-income groups. No newspaper wants to admit to itself, or to its advertisers, that it is read by the old and the poor, even when it *is*.

Meanwhile, in the world of education and the social services, Christian organizations which were founded to help, for example, the homeless or the addicted are increasingly finding that they cannot receive government or local authority aid, unless they relinquish outward symbols of faith, daily rituals expressing faith; there is sometimes pressure on them to relinquish aims and beliefs which are integral to their faith.[3]

And – most noticeably to anyone who takes an interest in discussions about how we raise our children – any mention of faith is avoided wherever the life of the family and parenting is discussed. Christianity, being the most popular faith, is normally referenced as a negative influence, a source of indoctrination or repression rather than of strength.

Human beings need opportunities to gather on a regular basis simply to express their relationship with the unseen. They need a framework for putting into words their feelings about things not normally talked about in the office, the workshop and the supermarket. People need, in short, the language of prayer, the structure of organized religion, a support system manned by personnel whose job gives them experience with human tragedy and crisis. They need a road map for their feelings about what is right and wrong.

If such a framework had not existed at all, it would have been extremely hard, for example, for people who sympathized with the family of Madeleine McCann, the child whose disappearance on a holiday in Portugal in May 2007 became a national *cause célèbre*, to show their feelings.

Being practising Christians, Madeleine's family had an automatic support system in place. There was a structure which made rallying round them an obvious and unproblematic thing to do. This structure was the presence of Anglican and Catholic churches in the area.

The believers and the tentative half-believers who took part in the Masses and prayers for Madeleine immediately after the child's disappearance did not believe their prayers could bring Maddie back from the dead, if indeed she was dead. Perhaps it looked to an outsider as though the worshippers inside the church thought their prayers could miraculously magic Madeleine back into their midst: I venture to suggest to this rather patronizing (though imaginary) outsider that worshippers, on the whole, are not that stupid.

But the worshippers did know, deep down, that their prayers would do something very important. They would help the McCanns and the rest of their family find a way of formulating their grief – an essential first step towards the future they must rebuild; and would help to give strength to those who needed it.

In the eyes of atheists, when the McCann parents attended a church service a few days after the disappearance of their daughter they did so only in a primitive bid to propitiate a cruel and vindictive God, to beg Him for the return of their child.

Once the story became more complex, with charges being brought against the parents themselves, then the strength they had gained from their faith was used against them: 'There is something odd about the energy of the McCanns. I would be confounded with grief . . .' hinted one BBC commentator[4] nastily as the Portuguese police indicated they had evidence against the parents. Even more hostile things began to circulate on the internet. In the eyes of atheists, the couple were, if innocent, flailing about misguidedly, begging an imaginary deity for help that could never come; or, if guilty, they were cynically using faith as a mask for their crime.

'*Imagine no religion*', runs the lyric of one of the world's most famous pop songs: John Lennon's *Imagine*. (The same song also contains the words 'Imagine no possessions' – words written, it has been justly pointed out, 'by a multi-millionaire with one temperature-controlled room in his Manhattan mansion just to store his fur coats'.[5])

But religion is what we *do*. It is a natural human activity. True enough, it can be used as an excuse for all kinds of unacceptable human activities; but so can science be used to create weapons of mass destruction as well as medicines and mobile phones. For every atrocity in the name of Christianity, there are a thousand acts of goodness which never make the headlines.

Non-religious people often talk of praying, or use the language of invocation (as in saying 'thank god') when they are in need or in distress. The language of religion is threaded through our culture and the language of Christianity is threaded through Western culture in particular. We ignore it at our peril: one day we will look round and find that the structure has gone. People can't pray well in an emergency if they have never had the experience of praying in a non-emergency.

Religion is our way of looking outside ourselves, our way of thinking about the 'otherness' of other people as well as the incomprehensible 'otherness' of God. It is a way of making us consider ourselves as part of a community, not as selfish, self-centred individuals.

G. K. Chesterton is often 'quoted' as saying that when a man ceases to believe in anything, he eventually *will* believe in anything. The 'quotation' is close in meaning to a number of the great English Catholic writer's *bons mots*, but it seems that if he did say it, it was not in any of his published works. He did, however, write that once a person began believing in a vague, New Age 'inner light' rather than in orthodox religion, then it was only a matter of time before the person began to worship himself – 'that Jones shall worship Jones'.

If you want to imagine no religion, imagine driving across Birmingham without a road map or road signs. If you do eventually get across Birmingham, it will be only by following what other people are doing, without any evidence that they know where they are going, or that they want to go the same way you do. You will get stuck in traffic jams you could have avoided. And you might end up going round in circles, or get lost altogether.

Notes

1. *Church Going in the UK*: survey published by Tearfund, 2007.
2. Office for National Statistics, 2002/3 data.

3. *Breakthrough Britain*, published 2007 by the Conservative Party's Social Justice Policy Group, *passim*.
4. Broadcasting House, BBC Radio 4, 9 September 2007.
5. *The Not so Fab Four*, Robert Elms, BBC Radio, London, 2006.

Ticking clocks – biological and otherwise 3

This is the day that the Lord has made;
let us rejoice and be glad in it.

Psalm 118.24

The first thing that a newly pregnant woman finds out about her baby is the 'due date', the day on which the baby is 'expected'. This date is fastened on by everybody involved – employers, grandparents, best friends, doctors – as the date around which everything else hinges. Before Due Date, the woman imagines herself as essentially still a child. She has nobody to think about and worry about but herself because her partner's role is – or should be – to protect and nurture her, and her relationship with her growing baby is so close that she need only take care of herself in order to take care of the baby.

After Due Date will come parenthood, responsibility; the centre of her life will be removed from its old position in her own body and relocated in a small, helpless infant with froggy little legs.

Some couples set themselves important goals to achieve before Due Date, either at work or in the form of home improvements, just as though on that special and particular day, all ability to wield a paintbrush, a telephone or a screwdriver would desert them for ever. They plan major changes to their homes, or move to a new home, which (of course) needs completely redecorating, and they turn the Due Date into a deadline before which all difficult tasks must be accomplished and after which some kind of total paralysis will descend.

As a childbirth educator and doula (that is, a woman who supports another woman before, during and after the birth of her child), the first thing I have to do when I meet a couple for the first time is to re-educate them about that 'due date'. It is in fact very unlikely that their baby will be born on that day. Only 4 per cent of babies are born on their due date. Most firstborns are born at least·a week afterwards. Some babies come early, and an awful lot come a bit later. In France a pregnant woman's 'due date' is calculated at 41 weeks', not 40 weeks' gestation.

The due date is no more than a midpoint in a period of time in which it is safe and optimal for a baby to be born, according to the World Health Organization's rubric. A baby born after the 40-week point is not 'late'. A baby is only 'late' if the mum is still pregnant at 42 weeks' gestation, and even then she may simply have an unusually long gestation period – what is unusual in terms of the norm is not necessarily unusual for that individual.

However often I repeat all this stuff, it goes straight over women's heads in mid-pregnancy. Some women just cannot help finding it immensely frustrating to be still pregnant after their due date: especially the kind of women who are never late for anything. These are the women who set themselves very high standards; women who hate to be caught unprepared for any eventuality; who drive themselves hard in their work lives. The women who manage their lives and the lives of many, who manage these well, yet still privately criticize themselves for not managing well enough. The highly organized women who order a large wooden cot with drop-sides about a year before their baby will be big enough to use it.

The last few days of pregnancy can be highly frustrating. The mum-to-be holds her breath expectantly every time she feels the slightest twinge, or she sits in her well-prepared lounge watching the clock hands turn round hour by hour. Every few minutes the phone rings – calls from friends who expect babies to arrive on their due date like parcels: 'haven't you had your baby YET?'

The feeling of wanting time to pass more quickly does not go away once a baby is born. 'You don't get much chance to lie on your tummy reading a book, do you!' exclaimed a friend (a non-mum) observing me with my first baby one day. It was a sharp observation because lying on my tummy reading a book had always been my pastime of preference; being naturally a physically lazy person I would always prefer reading a book to playing tennis or going on the swings. When you have a small baby, you do not have such freedom of choice.

That lack of freedom stretched out ahead of me – a life sentence of fussing over small children and not being able to lie on my tummy reading a book for hours on end. A life sentence of being patient and letting little ones go at their own snail-like pace. The very thought of it was enough to make me send the youngest off to a nursery at the earliest opportunity so that I could get back to the brisk pace of an office as soon as possible.

And yet 17 years later, I seem to have time to read any books I want, and my only problem in that respect is that I don't find it quite so comfortable to read a book lying on my tummy as I used to. Seventeen years later, I am at the airport waving goodbye to my youngest as she sets off to stay with a friend abroad for a fortnight, and a few days after that I am standing on the concourse at King's Cross Station watching a train carrying my eldest child away from me to work in Edinburgh for several weeks. I return to an unnaturally quiet house; the 15-year-old is reading the latest Harry Potter book and the 12-year-old is pursuing his own private agenda somewhere else in the house. Nobody seems to need me very much any more. The quietness is not quite melancholy; it is more a resigned air, a knowledge that now the party is over. I can choose, if I wish, to read a book lying on my tummy again.

And then – only then – I feel more than a twinge of regret for the times I used to long for the peace and solitude of an afternoon with a book rather than yet another couple of slowly passing hours playing with a toddler. How many times I tried to escape the fun and noise of my family. How many times I shied away from requests to play games, to go out for walks, because I had something else to do which seemed much more important. How many times I ducked out of opportunities to mess about with my children – and now find that the opportunities are nearly all gone, for gradually the children have stopped wanting me to mess about with them.

There is never as much time with your children as you think there is going to be. The biological clock ticks not only for the woman who longs for children and is in her late thirties, but also for those who have had children. Not only womanhood but parenthood and childhood tick away extraordinarily fast. Each stage a child reaches seems interminable when it is present ... and then, when it has gone, it seems to have passed with dizzying speed.

In his words as handed down to us in the Gospels, Christ called on his followers to live intensely in the moment, to focus on the day and not the morrow. He spoke, for example, of the man who piled up his bumper harvest, only to find that 'his soul was required of him' that night; of letting each day's trouble be sufficient to itself; of the lilies of the field that do not toil away for the future but are simply lovely to look at, however brief their span. All these powerful images are telling us to enjoy what we have; that only the moment in which we are living truly exists. Christianity is derided for its focus on the afterlife − but only by critics who have misunderstood the immediacy of Christ's message: it is what we do here, and now, how we treat the people right on our doorstep, which really counts.

'Every now and then I catch myself thinking I'll do it better next time round,' says a disappointed woman in one of Alan Bennett's monologues. There is no next time round and that is why there is a ticking clock, like a time-bomb, in the toolkit. All the other tools are useless without it because without the insistent reminder of the ticking clock, we will simply put off using them until tomorrow. And there may be no tomorrow.

A magic wand

4

The function of the imagination is not to make strange things settled, so much as to make settled things strange.

G. K. Chesterton

Ned Flanders, the irritatingly cheerful born-again Christian: No presents this year, kids. It's going to have to be an 'imaginary Christmas'.
Annoyingly angelic Flanders children: Hooray! Hooray! Imaginary Christmas!

The Simpsons, TV series created by Matt Groening

Lying next to the ticking clock of the previous chapter is something which every child asks for sooner or later: a magic wand. The ticking clock has a doleful rhythm, for sometimes only promises of things to come make the here and now bearable. Sometimes life as a parent can be very boring, very tiring, very routine and very frustrating. A magic wand is needed to make the *longueurs* of life with children bearable, or better yet, magical.

This particular kind of magic wand is not going to get the household chores done or conjure up a lottery win or a top-to-toe makeover. This magic wand is for putting the 'magic' back into everyday life; finding that sparkle that makes life wonderful. Walking to school in the rain is tedious, but when crocodiles lurk in every puddle and bears in the cracks of every pavement, how can life be dull?

The ability to see magic is what makes children such wonderful companions for adults, whose imaginative powers have been coarsened and dulled over the years by chores, deadlines and 'reality checks'.

'Not a day passes without seeing something in the children which pre-echoes heaven,' Sebastian, a father of three young children, told me. A media consultant, Sebastian confesses that he is constantly amazed at how much closer to God children are than adults. 'I don't feel I am teaching the children about faith – *they* teach *me* about faith rather than the other way around.' A child's imagination, the skill of seeing an exciting game lurking in the most everyday circumstances, is God-given and glorious, something to be adored – and to be kept in good working order by encouragement and praise, not by dull grown-up admonitions 'not to be silly'.

At the ordinary state school I went to, there was a protest in the classroom one day – around about when we were 14, an age for such things – from some girls who did not see why they had to do Religious Education. 'I don't believe there is anything in the world that you can't see, basically,' said their ringleader.

The same group of girls were also the least academically ambitious in the class. Their apathy was not confined to RE: it spread into all subjects on the curriculum and as far as they were concerned anyone who made an effort was a swot who did not understand what life was really 'about'.

What life was really 'about', according to them, was meeting boys, dancing, doing your nails, and that kind of stuff. In those days girls' magazines encouraged this narrow set of aspirations. The main thing in life was to get hold of the best-looking boy in the room, by whatever means. Their values were not wide-ranging, nor were their dreams high-reaching, and they were certainly unsullied by feminism. What is so disappointing is that, despite a certain amount of window dressing about girl power and assertiveness, today's girls' magazines (e.g. *Bliss*, *Sugar*) focus on exactly the same narrow range of goals: look good, be cool, get the right boy – just with more explicit sex added.

In one sense the girls who rebelled against RE were right: life for girls, for boys too, should be 'about' far more than studying. But a child who has never thought that there might be *unseen* wonders, or who has never stopped to look at the sheer miracle of everyday things, or who fails to ask not only how things work but why, is going around with blinkers on. Being closed to the possibilities of a spiritual world surely does not prepare a young mind well for the possibilities of the scientific world, and for the delights of knowledge purely for knowledge's sake.

Without wishing to sound too much like Ned Flanders, it is true that there is magic in everything. Here is a small selection of things which are, if you think about them for a minute, completely amazing and miraculous:

- The way drivers manoeuvre their way through crowded streets – and hit each other only now and again.
- The way trees move in the wind.
- Eggs.
- Babies learning to sit up and to crawl.
- Water.
- Flowers opening and closing even though, if you watch them, nothing seems to be happening.
- Tree roots which destroy house walls just by growing.
- Swimming.
- Putting on a blindfold and seeing how you can find your way around your home using only your sense of touch and hearing.

When the weather is cold and grey it is quite a challenge to find something 'magical' every day. Try it.

Children love ritual, and they love tradition. Creating your own traditions and rituals adds magic to everyday things: from Christmas Eve all the way down to the tooth fairy, we all have our little 'magic' games which increase in significance as the years pass. When children look back on birthdays, is it the presents that they remember – or is it the moment when Dad turned off the light switch and Mum came into the dark room with a cake ablaze with candles?

It is the magic of ritual that entrances children; they take a special delight in formal church services such as an Anglican High Mass or Roman Catholic Mass with incense and bells – as long as they are not stuck at the back of the church, and can see what is going on. A fascination with ritual is the first thing that attracts many children from purely secular backgrounds to religion of any kind. Ritual looks like magic. Magic makes things happen that we can only imagine. The child who has no contact with ritual will be desperately hungry for magic.

Ritual is about the here and now, the expression of the

moment. It is not a rehearsal, yet neither is ritual a performance. Rituals express things which otherwise are cumbersome to express. I have pointed out the part played by ritual for the tragic McCann family when their daughter went missing on holiday: but there are happier things for ritual to express as well, and within the framework of the ritual, the spontaneous finds its place.

My parish was saying goodbye to a young, newly ordained priest who had been working among us for a couple of years. He had made friends with pretty well everyone and worked very hard, so we expected a full church for his farewell Mass, and sure enough it was standing room only.

Suddenly at the end of Mass, and I am not sure we expected this, we found ourselves on our feet giving him a standing ovation lasting several minutes. I am not sure we expected to find our hearts so uplifted as he unwrapped his gifts (an icon, and an iPod – a euphonious combination). And I am not sure we expected to find the parish centre quite so amply filled as it was with good wine, home-cooked food and laughter afterwards.

Strange that a farewell can be so joyous; yet it was, because although we were saying 'goodbye' we were also affirming ourselves as a community through the ritual of the Mass. It was one of those moments when I wished I could parachute in a militant atheist author such as Richard Dawkins, and say, 'Look at what we are about! Joy, love and companionship! What's your problem?'

Imagination brings magic with it . . . and here is a very easy way of creating magic. Switch off the TV set – or get rid of it. It is alarming to see how quickly children find magic in everyday things if they do not have access to a television: it is as though the television invisibly drains away their creativity and drains away the magic with it.

The best holiday we ever had was a week in a big rented house in Scotland which we shared with another family whose three children were roughly of the same age as our own. Luckily we were three miles from the nearest road, so we let the children roam freely. Our two sets of siblings discovered a cave, formed a secret society, made a flag for it from a handkerchief and a stick and went slightly missing a couple of times. We, the parents, cooked, walked, read books and drank wine; we saw the children only to feed and scrub them. Instinctively, they had reverted to the behaviour of their E. Nesbit/Arthur Ransome antecedents, and fortunately for them their parents only became aware of the sheer 30-foot drop down from the bank of the stream to the rocks below quite late in the holiday: if we, the parents, had discovered this hazard early in the week, we would have been hovering over the children every day instead of letting them roam.

There was no TV in the house, nor a computer; no PlayStation or any other kind of electronic game. The children were forced to fall back on their own imaginations, and miraculously discovered that their imaginations were still in perfect working order. What I found inspiring was the speed at which the children could do this, the speed with which they rediscovered their secret magic wands and began using them to make spells again. My children are TV addicts, I might as well admit it. But within every TV addict a wand-wielding Harry Potter lurks.

Limiting TV is the best way of keeping your child's imagination active. Keep it in a locked cupboard (an ordinary wardrobe with lockable doors can easily be adapted to make a lockable TV cabinet, with drawers and space for peripherals and DVDs) or, if your children are young enough to accept it, insist on certain hours of the day when no TV is allowed. And if all else fails, take a deep breath and just turn it off.

Have a few ideas for things the child or children can get up to once the TV is off. Also be prepared for them to have some ideas of their own, and for these to be not quite what you had in mind. Don't go straight from being a TV-dependent parent to a 'helicopter parent' hovering over your child to make sure his or her time is filled with creative activities. Let them get a little bored: from boredom springs invention.

Not all TV is bad, and many computer games are enormously entertaining. But the trouble is they are so brilliant, so ingenious, that your child's own imagination simply seems redundant. Why bother, your child may ask, to invent whole worlds of one's own, when Sony, Microsoft and Nintendo have done all the work for us? Why bother, you may answer, to learn to walk when you can go everywhere by car? 'But that's bad for the environment,' your child may primly reply (the environment is the religion of the secular). 'Well, what about the environment inside your head?'

I used to think that once I'd laid down rules for limiting TV, then my battle with the monster would become easier, but in fact the battle never becomes easier: it just becomes more familiar.

A dog

5

As they were rejoining the crowd a man came up to him and went down on his knees before him. 'Lord,' he said, 'take pity on my son: he is demented and in a wretched state; he is always falling into fire and into water. I took him to your disciples and they were unable to cure him.' In reply, Jesus said, 'Faithless and perverse generation! How much longer must I be with you? How much longer must I put up with you? Bring him here to me.' And when Jesus rebuked it the devil came out of the boy, who was cured from that moment.

Then the disciples came privately to Jesus. 'Why were we unable to drive it out?' they asked. He answered, 'Because you have so little faith. In truth I tell you, if your faith is the size of a mustard seed you will say to this mountain, "move from here to there", and it will move; nothing will be impossible for you.'

Matthew 17.14–21

A dog? I don't mean a real dog . . . not unless you already own one. This particular item in the Christian parent's toolkit is a figurative, not literal tool. Dogs are, in the Christian West, the emblem of loyalty and unquestioning devotion and they give their name to a virtue: doggedness. They are treated with affection in Christian art and legend.

And even before Christian times, Homer told the story of Odysseus returning home, dishevelled and worn, from the Trojan War, and being rejected and unrecognized by all his household – except his faithful dog, Argus, who had looked out for him for twenty years. On seeing his master at last, Argus staggered from his wretched place on the dung-heap, greeted Odysseus with a feeble wag of the tail, and fell down dead at his feet. We can be sure there was not a dry eye in the house when Homer told this tale because everyone's heart is touched by such an image of doggy devotion.

A dog

St Jerome is traditionally depicted with a dog and a lion dozing at his feet as he studies. The thirteenth-century French saint Roch, who tended plague victims, was cared for by a faithful dog that brought him food every day after Roch contracted the plague from his own patients. When he returned home nobody recognized him, so (the legend says) he was thrown into jail for impersonating himself – where he and his dog continued to care for helpless prisoners. St Roch became the patron saint of dogs and dog-lovers.

Even though some cats try really hard to be nice, they can never quite match dogs, which are – provided they have not been perverted by cruel treatment by humans, or by equally cruel breeding practices also forced on them by humans – just the sweetest-natured animals in the world. 'If I have any beliefs about immortality, it is that certain dogs I have known will go to heaven, and very, very few persons,' said the American writer (and father of the one-liner) James Thurber.

And anyone who has ever known a dog knows how *dogged* they can be. A dog simply does not give up trying and he does not give up hoping. He carries on worrying away at that dry white bone, certain that if he keeps gnawing for long enough it will yield a tasty bit in the middle. He drops his ball at your feet and fixes you with an unwavering gaze, because he knows that if you were weak-willed enough to throw it for him once, you may well be foolish enough to throw it again. He does not mind how long it takes. He can wait.

He will watch the door all day while you are out, certain that if he looks at it hard enough it will open, certain that if he carries on emitting one sad bark every 3.5 seconds then eventually you will hear him and come home. It worked once, so it will work again – that's how a dog thinks. Dogs have faith: some might call it stupid faith, but it works insofar as it touches our hearts and makes us love them.

The man who brought his epileptic son to Jesus loved his broken, imperfect child – and loved him doggedly. He never gave up hope for him. He did not reject his son for failing to be the fine, upstanding, athletic, intelligent lad the man had hoped for before the child was born; his son was *his* son, so he devoted his life to him, and that was that. When Christ railed against the 'faithless and perverse' generation, he set their faith in contrast to the father's, who loved his son so much, and had so much faith, that he enabled the boy to be cured. Christ noted the man's faith, a faith that could move mountains. This father saw his boy not as a disability with a boy attached to it, but as his own boy, with a disability attached.

This level of parental love does indeed 'cure' disabilities because it semantically spirits the imperfections away: this level of parental love downgrades the most difficult problems to mere secondary attributes and at the same time sees not an imperfect person but a person who is as perfect in his own way as he can be. It makes the problems take second place, or lower, to the person who has them. The person might or might not get better; it makes no difference to the parental love. The parental love just carries on, dog-like.

This is not to say the father was limply fatalistic or passive about the boy's problems; on the contrary, he was absolutely certain that Jesus could help him; but it did not cross his mind to turn the boy out or reject him because of his affliction.

The parent's love never gives up. We cannot afford to give up. There is no room for impatience and giving up in the earliest days; impatience and giving up will quickly ruin the whole process. For example, if you want to breastfeed your newborn baby, you may need to have some patience and persistence in the first few hours, keeping the baby close to your body and giving the baby every opportunity to nuzzle and nestle by the breast until he works out how to get the nipple into his mouth by himself. But if you grab the baby by the scruff of the neck (as some older midwives occasionally do) and jam his face into the breast, he will be rightly alarmed and will clamp his mouth shut.

In fact, if this is your first baby, you might never have had to be so doggedly patient in your life. Patience and persistence are the qualities which young parents-to-be fear they lack most of all.

With all the development stages we have to be patient, watchful and dog-like in our devotion. It is unbearable. Walking down the road s-o-o-o slowly, our backs aching, as a toddler who has just learned to walk all by herself stops to examine every crack in every paving stone just because she's able now to do so. It takes a lot of patience and we all crack sometimes, giving in to the pressures of time or the temptation of sheer mind-numbing boredom; we scoop up the child and carry her swiftly down to the end of the road, or plonk her in her buggy for the rest of the way; and every time we do that, another tiny little opportunity for learning slips away.

Dog-like patience and devotion are required in waiting and watching as a small child figures out how to do a puzzle, even though you are longing to do it for her to save time. Letting her work out how to get food into her mouth, how to get her sock on all by herself ... and also helping her do these things not by doing them for her, but by showing her over and over again how to do them. This is how you get the spoon to your mouth ... this is how we fasten the shoe ... Mummy's done it, now *you* do it. These moments need extreme, dogged patience.

And when the small child is learning these small and vital skills you do not give up on her. Neither do you give up on her when she is a teenager. You doggedly keep showing her the right way of making friends, of judging between good influences and bad, of doing homework before going out clubbing, of making decisions about boys and alcohol and tobacco and drugs that are her decisions, formed by your teaching, and not formed by what her friends tell her to do. You keep on pointing out the way that you know works best, and eventually she will get it. But if you give up showing her, she will give up on ever getting it.

Why? Because if you give up on showing your child how to manoeuvre a spoon to her mouth, she will give up trying. If you give up letting her try to do a puzzle on her own, and do it all for her, she will never learn how to do it. When she is a teenager, the pattern does not change – it's just that the issues which make up the pattern get a bit bigger.

So don't give up asking your teenager dogged questions. Don't give up asking questions that you have a right to know the answers to – 'Where were you last night? ... Who were you with?' Any question you would not mind being asked yourself by your child, you have a right to ask your child. Be prepared to be a little bit dogged. After all, didn't the father of the prodigal son watch out doggedly for his son's return, day after day?

Doggedness does not imply aggression; the dog that repeatedly brings the stick back to his owner hoping for it to be thrown does not do so aggressively. He looks as friendly as he can, and wags his tail. Perhaps among the dogged parents, the parents who 'won't give up', are some of the most remarkable people of modern times. These are the people who, in the Sermon on the Mount, are blessed because they 'hunger and thirst for uprightness' (also sometimes translated as righteousness) – δικαιοσυνη: justice in Greek. They are people who fight for justice for their wronged or disregarded children; the parents who stick by a grown-up child who has committed a crime – such parents do not deny the crime, but continue to love and watch over their child. Or there are the parents who fight for the right to allow disabled children to receive a fair deal alongside other children once they have been born, even though society would prefer such children to be aborted.

To find that your new baby has a life-changing disability such as Down's syndrome is at first, I am told, like sinking into a bad dream from which you cannot get out; 'as though a grey veil has descended over your entire world', one mother told me. It feels as though where there was once a sunny, nicely planned life stretching out ahead of you, there is now a desert – a life of worrying and struggling to look after this strange person, this person you never wanted in your life anyway.

You think perhaps it is a bad dream, and you will wake up. Your feelings might turn to anger at the world, at God. You might even feel guilt, or just numb shock.

Yet, out of this horror, so many wonderful stories have been born; so many parents who discovered to their amazement that they could love their child as dearly as any other, and that their 'imperfect' child could bring them joy. Nobody's perfect, and no child is 'perfect'. A child is not a commodity to be chosen for its 'perfection'. Think about the families we all envy – the high achieving families where all the kids go to law college, are school sports heroes and routinely take the starring role in the school play – I am sure there is a family like this in your neighbourhood, your school, or that you hear of through your workplace. Do you think their children are perfect? Or might the parents just be very good at hiding their imperfections from your gaze?

Think now about the 'imperfect' child. Perhaps the 'imperfect' child is your child. The child's 'imperfections' – in other words, the ways in which this child deviates from an imaginary 'normal' that you built up in your imagination – are, in reality, the points at which your love as a parent comes through.

'If you do good to those who do good to you, what credit is that to you?' asks Christ in the Sermon on the Mount. Anyone can love a child who is talented, pretty, popular and who has a brilliant career ahead of her. Loving such a child is easy.

But it takes a parent to love a child who is a mass of problems. It takes a parent, a doggedly loving parent, to accept the child's imperfections, yet at the same time to hope that the child's problems can be overcome; it takes a parent to see that the child's imperfections do not define the child. It is in that place, the place of hope, where the imperfect is accepted, but not allowed to dominate, where that wonderful, dog-faithful father, the father of the epileptic boy cured by Jesus, is to be found.

A cat

6

In the course of their journey he came to a village, and a woman named Martha welcomed him into her house. She had a sister called Mary, who sat down at the Lord's feet and listened to him speaking. Now Martha who was distracted with all the serving said, 'Lord, do you not care that my sister is leaving me to do the serving all by myself? Please tell her to help me.' But the Lord answered: 'Martha, Martha,' he said, 'you worry and fret about so many things, and yet few are needed, indeed only one. It is Mary who has chosen the better part; it is not to be taken from her.'

Luke 10.38–42

It is fascinating to see how often in commentaries on this story a kind of war of the sexes takes place. You can tell a lot from people, especially priests, not so much by the way they side with Martha or Mary but by the form which their praise and criticism takes.

A certain kind of male preacher, seeking to be trendily anachronistic, disparages Martha for 'fussing over the washing-up'. Wrong. It was not the washing-up, the aftermath of the meal, which concerned Martha – that could have waited for a while; it was the serving of the meal that occupied her. If Martha had not been busy, nobody would have got anything to eat, including Jesus and Mary.

A feminist perspective on the story disparages Martha almost as much by portraying her as a poor misunderstood victim, trapped in her domestic chores. This standpoint stems from a deep-seated contempt for domestic chores and, by association, for those who have no choice but to do them, whether for themselves or for others. The feminist perspective sides thoroughly with Mary, and the anti-feminist perspective consequently takes up the gauntlet and sides with Martha. 'I always feel sorry for Martha,' is a muttered comment I have heard more than once from women, as though Martha were unfairly treated by Jesus.

Christ told Martha that Mary had chosen 'the better part'. I do not believe he was disparaging Martha's work in the home; his parables are full of images of daily work of all kinds. Jesus shows no sign of being in the slightest bit interested in arranging some kind of hierarchy of men's work over women's work. The parable of the lost drachma is told in tandem with the parable of the lost sheep (Luke 15) and both are preludes to the story of the lost or prodigal son. The three parables build up to a climactic image of God's boundless love and mercy.

Our male-dominated Western civilization has chosen to produce far more artistic representations of the story of the lost sheep than of the lost drachma; in Jesus' telling of them there is no hierarchy: he gives the woman's story (the lost drachma) equal weight to that of the man's (the lost sheep).

Mary, too, had her own domestic chores; all women of her time did, and we are not necessarily to think she despised or neglected them. She simply had a better sense of priorities and of the 'here and now', and she knew that listening to Jesus was, at that time and place, more important.

The contrast Jesus drew was not between domestic chores and intellectual pursuits. Jesus makes no commentary on the role of women here, on feminism or any such temporal debates. There are plenty of male Marthas around. Jesus' loving criticism of Martha centres on the problem that she is worrying about a lot of things, when 'few are needed, indeed only one'. There is an echo of the hedgehog and the fox of the ancient Greek poet Archilochus: 'The fox knows many things, but the hedgehog knows only one big thing.' But rather than introducing foxes and hedgehogs, it seems more in keeping to observe that Martha is a dog-like person, and Mary is more cat-like.

One cat and one dog shared my childhood. The two animals had completely different ways of expending energy.

The dog, if he was not being walked briskly round the countryside, amused himself by trotting up and down on the grass verge outside our house, asking to be let into the house, trotting round to the back door, asking to be let out, trotting round to the side gate which he hoped to find open, and round to the front door again. The cat, on the other hand, sat and sat and sat. I have known more energetic cats, and less energetic dogs, but I have a lasting impression that cats always behave as though they have to husband their energy, save it up, whereas dogs, though faithful and patient and untiring, behave as though they need to use up their energy as quickly as possible.

When my own cat had kittens, and especially when the four kittens began wobbling about on their furry little spaghetti legs, it was instructive to watch her with them. She did not chase them needlessly around the room or fuss over them. She lay where she could see them, perfectly still, and kept her eyes on them. She was conserving her energy.

Stillness is a great art. Students of hypnotherapy – who have to learn, first of all, to go into a hypnotic state themselves by becoming very relaxed, in order to know for themselves the state of mind to be produced in their clients – find that it does not come easily to everyone. Students of meditation report the same kind of initial problems. Yet in both disciplines, there are virtually no students who fail to reach some level of hypnosis, or some level of meditation, eventually. The craft of being relaxed and allowing one's body to rest is a cat-like craft, and some of us are dog-like people, and need to practise to learn. So here is another figurative tool for the toolkit; along with the metaphorical dog, there is an imaginary cat, to teach us how to be still and not to waste our energy.

The cat's great gift is his detachment. He watches, and he does not get fussed about details. One slightly cat-like (insofar as she is a person of poise and elegance) friend of mine has two teenage children and one little one still at primary school. She is very 'in touch' with her children, and they confide in her. She often reminds me of a mother cat when she is with her children, for she never fusses over them though she always knows exactly where they are and what they are doing. Cat mothers allow children to explore their world and they accept that such exploration might mean the home is not exactly a *Homes & Gardens* photo feature, for a few years. When a cat mother's kids make a terrible mess in the kitchen after an adventure with pastry, the cat mother puts more fervour into enjoying the jam tarts that have resulted than into her complaints about the mess.

Cat mothers do not invade their children's space. They do not open their mail or sneak around in their bedrooms opening diaries marked 'very very VERY private'. They do not make small matters such as their children's different taste in hairstyles and clothes into major issues. My cat-mother friend once observed that 'allowing space around stuff' was crucial to living with teenagers.

February 5th is St Agatha's Day. On this day, in medieval France, women were supposed to take a holiday and do no work. Any woman who was caught doing any chores on that day would be confronted by an angry cat, said to be St Agatha in disguise. How poor St Agatha, who was martyred because she refused to submit to a forced marriage (and, as a punishment for her refusal, was sent into a brothel, raped and sexually abused), has got herself mixed up in this role, so at odds with her tragic life, is one of those mysteries of the Church nobody ever explains.

It is a jokey legend, a way of acknowledging that the traditional observance of Sunday as a day without work rarely extended to the women of the house. Behind it lies the recognition that the person who runs a home often has to be gently cajoled into finding her off-switch, her inner cat mother, because she is so conditioned to a life of constant drudgery and fussing that she has had little practice in finding 'time to stand and stare'.

St Agatha's Day is for the Marthas of the world. In the story of Martha and Mary, Martha is a person who does not have an off-switch, whereas Mary has found hers and is not afraid to use it. Some Marthas, in fact, need a St Agatha's Day at least once a week – a true Sabbath, to encourage them to find their off-switch. It is important for energetic, bustling people to calm down and enjoy the here and now, to listen and to think, and to be still for a while, praying and reading or even just enjoying the feel of the warm sun on their skin.

Even if they only do it for fear of being chased by an ancient Roman martyr disguised as an angry moggy.

Bouquets and compost 7

A man had a fig tree planted in his vineyard, and he came looking for fruit on it but found none. He said to his vine-dresser, 'For three years now I have been coming to look for fruit on this fig tree and finding none. Cut it down: why should it be taking up the ground?' 'Sir,' the man replied, 'leave it one more year and give me time to dig round it and manure it: it may bear fruit next year; if not, then you can cut it down.'

Luke 13.6–9

If our children are our garden, we need to invest in a good mulch.

I am not advocating that you tip a bag of garden manure over your children, however much you may occasionally feel so frustrated by them that this would seem like a pleasant way of spending an afternoon. Rather, I am talking about love, praise and attention – the best growing material known to gardeners, and one calculated to produce the most surprising, abundant and even delicious fruit.

The owner of the fig tree was frustrated by its disappointing performance. Likewise, children are not always instantly rewarding. Not all toddlers learn to speak at the same time, and some may not utter the torrent of charming words that their parents hope for as quickly as their friends' children do.

When our babies are born, we look at them with such glowing pride that our imaginations begin to run riot. This baby, we tell ourselves, will be captain of the team, top of the class, the star of the show. This baby will always be popular and will be first in every race on sports day.

Our imagination continues to work overtime, as we see ourselves on the sideline, jumping up and down with excitement as the tall, handsome child easily breasts the finishing tape ... we imagine ourselves proud and serene in an audience of wildly cheering parents as our child takes the fifth curtain call at the end of the school musical ... and in the final scene, the one with the smiling young person walking back from the graduation ceremony dais in academic gown and mortar-board, we are the smartly dressed parents towards whom the star student is headed.

Yet there are more supporting actors and extras in every movie than there are stars, and all those supporting actors and extras have parents, too. All those parents, the vast majority, must stand and clap while other people's children take the prizes. On the basis of statistics alone, parent fantasies are highly unlikely to be fulfilled. Not all children can be above average.

Have you ever noticed how people who believe in reincarnation always turn out to have been grand public figures in earlier lives? An awful lot of people are convinced they were Roman generals but isn't it odd how nobody seems to remember being, in a previous life, the 34th unfortunate Roman legionary in the 28th row of the 17th legion on a wet and miserable march across Northern Europe?

It is the same with parental fantasies. The fantasies of success and glory do not prepare us very well for the pain of seeing our child come last in the race – or even somewhere in the crowd around the middle. The fantasies do not prepare us well for when the child struggles at school, or merely fails to shine; misses out on the scholarship, does not quite get the college place or the job he or she really wanted but instead has to make do with second, even third best. The fantasies of the parent-to-be are founded on a major misconception: the mistaking of ambition for love. It is when we find ourselves loving the imperfect child, or the child who never amounts to anything very much, that we truly realize the power of love.

In an earlier chapter, we considered the father who brought his epileptic son to Jesus, and the man's dogged and hopeful love for his child. In our own time, the award-winning sports writer Simon Barnes has written movingly of life with his Down's syndrome son, Eddie.

When a prenatal scan indicated that Eddie had Down's syndrome, Barnes wrote, 'the hospital very kindly offered to kill him for us',[1] an offer the parents declined. After his birth the baby needed a series of heart operations. Caring for a Down's child is difficult, exhausting, time-consuming and never ending.

Yet, as Barnes has discovered, none of this is really a 'burden' because love is never a burden. Tasks undertaken for love are never as irksome as they would be if undertaken for someone you don't care very much about. It is love for one's child which transforms an ordinary person into a miracle.

As he wrote, in an essay for *All About Us*, a book compiled to mark the 60th anniversary of the charity Mencap, which supports the mentally handicapped and their families:

> The human imagination can do many extraordinary things. But we can't imagine love. Or perhaps I mean loving: love as a continuous state; one that carries on in much the same way from day to day, changing and growing with time just as people do. The great stories of literature are about meeting and falling in love, about infidelity, about passion. They are seldom about the routines of married life and having children.

A society in which women discuss how to find the 'perfect' man in the same tones as they discuss finding the 'perfect' handbag must find it hard to understand how parents can be entirely happy with an 'imperfect' child. A society which treats any kind of human frailty as something that can be operated on, drugged or educated out of existence must find it hard to accept that the imperfect, even the grossly imperfect, might have as much right to life, education, housing, healthcare and – above all – love as the perfectly perfect.

Yet once the initial shock of disability has worn off, the parents of any disabled child will tell you, the power of love sweeps in and fills every crevice, nook and cranny of your soul. 'I'm not a saint, just a parent,' says Simon Barnes. He is only one of many millions of parents of 'imperfect' children who would say the same.

'Love and work are the cornerstones of our humanness', said Sigmund Freud. This is especially true for parents. As Barnes writes, 'the love that moves the sun and other stars is also the love that makes the toast and other snacks'. Looking after children is hard work but love makes it easy. Looking after children who need a lot of looking after is even harder work . . . but again, love makes it easy. 'Love is the most humdrum thing in life, the only thing that matters, the thing that is forever beyond the reach of human imagination.'

Most children can be very hard work at times. They don't need to have Down's syndrome or any disability to be worrying, problematic, dependent or frighteningly vulnerable. They may falter and be fragile at any time. They may get into scrapes and fall out with their friends. They may neglect their homework, get terrible school results and drop out altogether. They may get mixed up in crime, drugs, violence.

These are the 'barren fig tree' moments of parenthood. These are the moments when we might be tempted, like the man in Jesus' story, to cut off the connection, hand the problem over to social services and shrug. But by the miracle of love, we don't do any such thing. We do what the gardener says we should do: we grab an extra bag of compost off the shelf, and give that needy tree yet more love, all the love we can find. The more barren the fig tree, the uglier and pricklier its branches, so the more it needs that love – and it needs that love to be seen, shown, displayed and made public.

By a strange irony it is sometimes the most caring parents who find it hardest to give praise and show affection. Parents with very high standards – standards of behaviour, academic achievement, success – can be really difficult to cope with because they can never quite make praise sound genuine whereas their criticism is always genuine. Children pick up insincerity so easily.

The competitive streak which fuelled the new parent's birthing-room fantasies – 'this child will be the best at everything . . .' – is the same competitive streak that leaves many young people from high-achieving families feeling they are never going to be good enough . . . whatever they do.

It does not come naturally to us to offer a stubborn child or a recalcitrant teenager the occasional verbal bouquet of flowers, and it sometimes can be hard to find specific things to give praise for. Praise is best when specific – not 'I think you're wonderful' but 'I really like the way you picked up your towel off the floor this morning'; 'Thank you for setting the table'; 'thanks for taking out the rubbish' (even when you had to ask them to do it five times!).

When your communication levels are low, it can be hard for such moments of praise not to sound sarcastic, hard to bite one's tongue and hold back the cutting comment one longs to add as a sting in the tail: *'thanks so much* for taking out the rubbish ... *eventually'*.

'We like sitting round the dinner table,' a Christian mother of five told me, 'and saying one thing in turn about the person next to you that you have appreciated that week. We do this on Sundays after church. It's pretty good for settling sibling squabbles.'

Genuine praise comes straight from the heart, straight from the love that lives in there. A good rule of thumb, especially if you are one of those parents to whom positive remarks do not come easily, is to try to say five positive things to your child – or your partner, or your friend, or your work colleague, for all relationships can be improved by honest praise – for every one negative thing you feel you can't avoid saying. Can't manage five? How about two?

For some of us, a ratio of just one positive to every negative remark would be an improvement! Showering a child with love is not easy when you have felt disappointed in that child. But the more love you pour on, then the finer will be the fruit which your love bears.

Note

1.   'I'm not a saint, just a parent', reprinted in *The Times*, 13 November 2006.

Invisible string and a key

8

And at once the cock crowed, and Peter remembered what
Jesus had said ... And he went outside and wept bitterly.

Matthew 26.75

All women become like their mothers; if this is their tragedy, as the
character in whose mouth this particular Wildean *bon mot* first
found breath[1] seems to think, then it has very little to do with what
kind of mother the woman had. The daughters of terrible mothers
understandably do not wish to turn into their mothers; but it is an
oddity of human nature that the daughters of exemplary mothers
almost always feel the same way. Even the daughters of delightful,
brilliant, wise and virtuous mothers are known to clap a horrified
hand to their mouths at the sudden thought: '*I sound just like my
mother*'.

If you have ever had that thought cross your mind as some well-
worn turn of expression crossed your lips, you are not alone. If you
have ever felt first a twinge of horror when your child says, 'You
sound just like Granny', followed by a twinge of guilt – what's
Granny done to deserve me being so desperate NOT to be like
her? – you are not alone.

By the time we are adults, we want to believe that we have
broken away from our parents enough to develop our own style,
and in particular our own parenting style. Imitation of one's parents' way of bringing up children – the use of tradition – is considered to be a fault these days, where it once was considered a
virtue: I don't hold any brief for either view, but I do note that
Jesus asked us literally to *turn aside from our families*. The Gospels are
spiced with a number of such peppery commands. The Jesus of St
Luke's Gospel strikes me as particularly short-tempered, forever
exploding with exasperation. His warning to us that by following

35

Him we may 'set father against son' and divide families may make us blanch with dismay.

But He is not telling us to dishonour our parents, to stop loving them or to hurt their feelings. I believe that he is asking us not to step neatly into our parents' way of doing things just because this is 'the done thing'. Neither is he telling us to rebel against our parents purely for the sake of rebellion. A regard for tradition is at once a central concept of our faith – and at the same time a pitfall for the unwary. Christ warned us against blindly following tradition simply because it has been handed down to us on a plate by our parents and families. He said that we must turn against our families in order to follow him. One way of reading his words is to see that we must challenge everything our families taught us, test every precept and saying for its truth; we must not accept everything we are taught simply because we are taught it.

Do not believe in traditions because they have been handed down for many generations, the Buddha is recorded as saying. A tradition's venerable age may endear it to a historian, but does not *necessarily* commend it as a way of life. To find Jesus Christ advocating turning against the traditions of our families might be particularly hard to swallow for those of us of a conservative nature, who prefer the tried and tested rather than the modern and untested.

Christ's meaning is that we have to find our own way, and it may turn out to be exactly the way our parents chose – but we have to find it and choose it for ourselves. Children have to test the traditions, words of wisdom, rules of thumb and other handed-down bits of knowledge which their parents bequeath to them, simply to find out if they are still genuinely roadworthy.

Which is why when we are young, our parents may often be seen sitting on their hands and biting their lips in agony, watching us learning from mistakes they remember making themselves years ago ... and it is also why when we are parents, we cannot wrap our own children in cotton wool and protect them from their own mistakes. So instead of wads of cotton wool to protect children from the mistakes we made once upon a time, all we need is a ball of invisible string, which is *experience*, and a *key*, which is the freedom to make mistakes of our own in our own time.

Invisible string and a key

Child safety experts advise parents who take small children to adventure playgrounds never to try to help children climb up. The child climbs best on her own; unaided, she will climb as far as her ability allows her and no further; if she got up there by herself, she can get down by herself.

The truly helpful parent is not hovering close by offering the child their hand, but instead stands near making cheerful, encouraging noises with hands firmly rammed in pockets. An invisible string attaches itself from the parent to the child – the invisible string of watchfulness, of many-times repeated warnings and many-times repeated reminders to 'be careful'. But the invisible string always allows the child the freedom of choice.

This rule seems to apply to so many areas of parenting and the dangers do not get smaller. The first time I sent my oldest child away to a summer job I stuffed into his suitcase a 17-page dossier of 'do's and don'ts' which I had compiled specially for him. He told me firmly that he had no intention of reading the dossier, because he already knew how to look after himself. I simply could not believe this: after all, didn't I know better than him about – oh, about practically everything? Was he not barely more worldly-wise than the day I gave birth to him? It was a shock to find that he could, in fact, cope without me. I do not know if he read the dossier, but I suspect he threw it away. His chilly response to my attempt at long-distance mothering was his way of telling me that the invisible string protecting him was there, in place, doing its job – but he had become aware of it sooner than I had.

Scattered around London are several front-door keys belonging to our house; left on buses, left in school bags, even put down on park benches. . These are keys we have entrusted to our children at various times over the years. Once a child in our family reaches secondary school age, he or she is deemed old enough to go to school unaccompanied, and is duly given his or her own set of front door keys. Regular as clockwork, within a month of being entrusted with keys, the child loses them. And the school-locker key along with it, naturally.

And when that happens? The parents tut-tut in an exasperated manner, and wail and rail a bit, and then go out and get some more keys cut. And we hand those keys to the child again and give them another chance. We repeat the warnings, and eventually they sink in ... eventually the key becomes tied to the child's pocket with invisible string made up of habit and practice.

In medieval Christian art, every important person has a distinguishing feature, something they are holding or wearing that tells the observer, who probably is illiterate, which saint he is meant to be looking at. Everybody has a 'logo', if you like – to help identify him or her. St Peter is always represented with a key, the key to the Kingdom of Heaven which Jesus entrusted to him (Matthew 16.13–23).

Once entrusted with the key, Peter proceeded to either mess up or put his foot in it at every opportunity. He tried to walk on the water and nearly drowned himself because he suddenly doubted. He tried to start a fight in the Garden of Gethsemane. Lastly, he panicked after Jesus' arrest and tried to pretend he did not know his Lord. St Peter is the nearest thing to a comic turn in the Gospels – on the night of Jesus' arrest, one can almost imagine him desperately trying to put on a posh city accent to disguise his thick regional one – and his mistakes are more compelling in narrative terms than almost any other acts of the disciples.

Yet Jesus chose Peter, for all his blundering, as his rock, because Peter's heart was right. He gave him the key, the responsibility to decide which way the work of Christ should go. In other words, he trusted Peter's ability to learn from his mistakes, to recall what he had learned and to pray deeply enough to be able to lay his fingers on the invisible string of his Master's intentions, the thread leading on to the right path through the labyrinth.

Note

1. **Lord Illingworth**: All women become like their mothers. That is their tragedy.
   Mrs Allonby: No man does. That is his.

   A Woman of no Importance

Masks, adult-sized

9

A stage, where every man must play his part ...
William Shakespeare, The Merchant of Venice

It was one of those hot, tetchy shopping afternoons when all six
people in the family wanted to go in different directions. We had
set off with a short, achievable list of goals – a birthday present for a
friend, something pretty for my teenage daughter to wear, an
essential widget for my husband's computer. We had a deadline for
getting home but had no worries about meeting it.

I should have known things would turn out badly when it took
me 15 minutes to find a parking space large enough for our seven-
seater car. Before we had even parked, one of the voices from the
back seat announced that it wanted to go off by itself for a browse
in W. H. Smith's. Another voice piped up and said it didn't want
to go there, but would rather go to Top Shop on its own if we
didn't mind. Before I knew what had happened we had split up
into three different parties ... and not all the parties had mobile
phones with them.

Convening a rendezvous should have been easy – we just had to
meet at the car at an agreed hour. But some members of my family
have a dim sense of the passage of time and others refuse to wear a
watch. And, remember, we had a deadline for getting home – it
was one of those days when I regret having said to some friends,
'Oh, just come round any time after five – we are always in on
Saturday afternoons ...'

In the end, what should have been a very straightforward
shopping expedition ended with me charging, hot, red-faced and
furious, up and down the high street trying to lasso my family back
under my control as I glimpsed them at brief intervals through gaps
in the crowds which thronged the hot, dirty London pavement.

Is there anything more embarrassing than being spotted in a

public place by someone you know, while you are in the act of yelling uncontrollably at your children? Most of us want to give the impression of being in control, calm and collected; perfectly well-adjusted parents. So I did not feel too sanguine when a few weeks later a client said sweetly, 'Oh I saw you in the high street a little while ago. You were shouting at your daughter, I think . . .'

I was mortified. If as I do you deal professionally with pregnant women all the time, you try your hardest to present an air of professional calm and motherly warmth in which clients are supposed to feel secure and relaxed. Being caught snapping my child's head off wasn't part of the plan. I recalled the day with a futile racking of my memory to check if I'd been swearing . . . my mask had slipped, and I had been caught out.

A mother who left her two daughters, aged six and nine, standing in the rain on the side of a Northumberland motorway found herself in court charged with neglect. The girls had been quarrelling about shoes; their mother had, after a long and difficult day, finally snapped and told them both to get out. Then she drove off, leaving the astonished children on the hard shoulder.

This story brought back for me another memorable day. My brother (aged ten) and I (aged five) were quarrelling so much in the car that my mother drew the car to a halt and ordered us both to get out and walk home. I am not charging my mother with a 1960s version of the motorway dumping: we only had a mile to walk on a very quiet country lane, which we knew like the back of our hand. The effect, however, was salutary. I must have either burst into tears or looked as though I might, because my clearest memory of the walk home is of my brother being unusually kindly and genuinely protective. I think he might even have summoned the courage to face what must be the average ten-year-old boy's worst nightmare – holding his little sister's hand.

When we got home – it was probably the middle of summer but my memory insists that it was growing dark and cold as we trudged up to the garden gate – there were hugs and probably cups of hot cocoa. For a scary moment, our mother's mask had slipped – she was no more the rational, patient, forbearing and responsible adult we had always known her to be, but suddenly an irrational, pet-ulant creature, as much subject to whims and flights of temper or fancy as we children ourselves. I do not think we squabbled for quite some time – probably at least a couple of days – after that. As for my mother: she was undoubtedly deeply relieved to see us both at the front door, meek but safe – I cannot remember if such relief showed on her face, so perhaps by that time she had rearranged the mask once more.

Parenting gurus of the twenty-first century set very high standards of behaviour. I mean parental behaviour, not children's. The parenting icons who seem to have the most success are fierce, rather unforgiving perfectionists such as Jo Frost, star of the immensely successful TV series *Supernanny*, or Gina Ford, author of *The Contented Little Baby Book*, whose rigid timekeeping advice has sold millions of copies. This generation of advice-givers puts much emphasis on the calm, rational mask which they insist is necessary to wear throughout the process of good parenting. Never raise your voice. Never lose control. Never miss out on the mid-morning nap or alter the bedtime routine. Think before you talk. Be rational and reasonable at all times. Project confidence and certainty in your authority. And never, never, never lose your temper.

This kind of advice is what Christians call a 'counsel of perfection'. It is an ideal to be aimed for, not to be attained at all costs. A parent who lets the mask slip a little now and then may still be a good parent, or what the parenting gurus of an older, more relaxed generation called 'a good enough parent'. Like hemlines, parenting fashions are subject to sudden reversals of fortune. The parents of the 1960s and 70s were encouraged by their gurus to let it all hang out, to outlaw the idea of reining in emotion, to scorn their own parents' habits of 'putting on a brave face' or maintaining a stiff upper lip. Now the stiff upper lip is right back in fashion as our child-rearing gurus drum into clients and TV audiences alike the importance of maintaining PERFECT CONTROL at ALL TIMES.

The problem with a counsel of perfection is that unless you recognize it as such, it rapidly degenerates into a counsel of despair. It is impossible to keep that mask up all the time. And who, anyway, wants to be brought up by a person wearing a mask? Who wants to be brought up by someone who is constantly hiding how they feel? Who wants to be raised by a robot with a Smiley face glued to the front of its head?

Short of putting children in actual danger, the occasional moment of mask-slippage cannot be very harmful. It is scary to see a parent in an uncontrollable rage; but surely it is far less scary to see a parent stomp off in a bad temper to reappear five minutes later saying 'sorry'? If our children never see us recovering our poise and equilibrium after a momentary wobble, how will they learn to do so themselves?

Yet our faith tells us that there are times when we should wear a mask, and when wearing the mask helps us not only in our relationships but in our inner lives as well. A wise man once said to me when I complained that I was finding it hard to 'feel' devout, 'Try playing the part.'

'Playing the part' of a devout Catholic mother sounds more like advice from Central Casting than from a real-life friend, I thought at first. I don't want to be some kind of movie villain hiding my evil intent behind a mask of religious fervour. No thanks. We Catholics get quite enough bad publicity of that kind as it is, what with *The Da Vinci Code* and the steady stream of aggressively anti-Catholic movies which pours out of Hollywood.

However, modern psychologists tell us that if we smile and look happy, we will begin to feel happier. It sounds trite but it does work. If you smile, people tend to smile back at you, which makes you feel better. So if you play the part of the happy person, you begin, gradually, to slip into the habits of thought which are natural to a happy person: being positive, optimistic, being glad to see people and so on. You find that your happiness is bounced back at you by others, who become habitually glad to see you: your own self-esteem is thus built up.

Likewise, when you don't feel like doing the truly Christian thing – the forgiveness, the turning of the other cheek, the loving of one's enemies – if you just 'play the part' and 'do it' anyway, then you may find yourself doing the right thing, and getting the right result – and you may also find yourself growing into the part as you go along.

Let's take a classic workplace situation – where there is a colleague who irritates you beyond endurance. 'Playing the part' of the good Christian, you may start out with a half-hearted 'OK, I am trying to think compassionate and positive thoughts about nasty old Mrs X, who pokes her nose into my work and makes my life a misery, but this isn't really me' attitude. But in time (if you are persistent) you may end up with a surprising discovery – that this indeed is you. You realize that you are capable of feeling real compassion for nasty old Mrs X. You begin to wonder what made her so nosy and disagreeable, to wonder what past pain or sorrow has made her the way she is . . .

We become what we want to be by doing it, and what we keep on doing leads us to what we become. In the 1990s there was a rather sentimental but unforgettable film called *Mr Holland's Opus*. Richard Dreyfuss played a classically trained composer who takes a job as a high school teacher to make ends meet while writing his symphonic masterpiece, a work of genius which, he imagines, will astound critics and touch the hearts of millions.

As the years go by, Mr Holland's teaching skills grow and develop, yet the masterpiece, pushed aside by other worries and disappointments, proceeds at a snail's pace. Finally, nearing retirement, Mr Holland has to accept that his true masterpiece dwells not between the covers of a musical score, but in the thousands of youngsters whom he has taught, encouraged and occasionally bullied into enjoying music over the years.

So while he thought he was 'going through the motions' of being a good high school music teacher, Mr Holland woke up one day to discover that he had mutated into a very good high school music teacher beloved of his pupils; his pupils themselves were his *magnum opus*. Psychologists tell us that if we go through the motions of being happy, some of the happiness can rub off on to our inner selves and we can become happier. If we 'go through the motions' of being good parents, we might wake up one day to discover that we have been pretty good parents after all.

The part of the good parent is a complex one that has been rewritten many times by many scriptwriters, not all of whom were following the same plot. But Christ's advice to parents is extremely simple and is the same advice he applies to everyone: we must love, forgive, love, forgive and love some more, for ever and ever. And for ever – when you are a parent – really does mean for ever.

We must always keep the door open for the returning prodigal, even when we are longing to slam it shut in the prodigal's face. Even – perhaps especially – when the prodigal is a surly and ungrateful teenager.

Putting on a mask is akin to putting on a brave face, an act of self-protection which many women perform in the most literal sense. A client of mine who was pregnant several days beyond her due date found the waiting very stressful and even broke down in tears a few times, though she had been sunny, serene and glowing throughout her pregnancy until that point. I spoke to her every day and found her mood swung violently, as will often happen, and then she would dry her tears, take a deep breath and go and put on her makeup. 'I've been and put my face on, and that always makes me feel better,' she would say with a smile. This young woman felt that slapping on the eye makeup and the lipstick did her a world of good – it was not only her mask, but her armour.

A smile can be armour. It is not good if the smile hides a desperate need to be loved, a wounded heart or a damaged soul, but it can be armour against more humdrum problems. Putting on a brave face, or a patient face, or a happy face, or a forgiving face, is the first step to feeling braver, and *feeling* braver is the first step to *being* braver. The trick with the mask, as with all armour, is that it must be easily removed for cleaning and maintenance, and not glued permanently to our faces. The mask must be something we can put on when we require it – and take off when it is time to reveal the truth which God sees all the time.

Masks for children

10

Laugh, and the world laughs with you; Weep, and you weep alone; For the sad old earth must borrow its mirth, But has trouble enough of its own.

Ella Wheeler Wilcox,
American poet and 'free thinker' (1850–1919)

The Christian faith has been the moral petrol running the motor of Western civilization for a very long time. If we don't keep filling up the tank, the motor will career along for a while, running on empty, but it will eventually grind to a halt. Faith has been and can continue to be immensely creative, producing interesting and profound answers to questions about human problems, from the great to the small.

Let us take an issue which is so normal, so everyday, that it hardly rates as a moral dilemma: shyness. The shy child who won't talk to strangers, the teen who won't go to parties, the blushing and tongue-tied young adult who is hopeless with the opposite sex or in job interviews – they are all familiar characters. There is one such person in most families (and some families seem to be made up of nothing but shy people). Shyness is not a great social issue. It is not on a par with family breakdown, drugs, the debt crisis, famine, AIDS or global warming. Yet when you have a child who is shy, it is painful. The most common adjective attached to 'shyness' is probably 'crippling' and certainly it can limit a child's life like a disability.

Jesus was not a shy person. Not even the experience of getting a chilly reception ('They said, "This is Joseph's son, surely?" ' – Luke 4.22) when he preached in his home town seems to have bothered him. Throughout the Gospels Jesus has a self-awareness which is mystical and profound; the Gospel writers have him hinting at the future, at his divinity. This self-awareness is just that – awareness of his self and his meaningfulness.

A cripplingly shy child or young adult, on the other hand, suffers not from being self-aware, but from being too self-conscious: too ready to believe that everyone is looking at her, and that as soon as she walks into a room, everyone is looking at her critically.

It is a paradox that while the shy child has a very low opinion of herself, she may at the same time be very bad at taking criticism. At anything she sees as a negative remark, she will either explode into a raging sulk and storm off to her room, or sink even further into a cycle of self-hatred ... or both. Lack of self-esteem often looks very like arrogance. Having very low self-esteem is rather like having very bad sunburn; the skin is so raw and tender that the lightest touch becomes agonizingly painful, so one protects oneself, desperately, with a show of aggression and pride. Interaction with other people is the most painful kind of contact of all on this, the poor inflamed skin.

In the Gospel of Luke we find Jesus constantly interacting with other people. He sees them, and thinks about them, interprets their actions:

> Then some men appeared, carrying on a bed a paralysed man whom they were trying to bring in and lay down in front of him. But as the crowd made it impossible to find a way of getting him in, they went up on to the flat roof and lowered him and his stretcher down through the tiles into the middle of the gathering, in front of Jesus. *Seeing their faith* he said, 'My friend, your sins are forgiven you.' (Luke 5.18–20)

We often see things in Luke's Gospel almost through Jesus' own eyes: 'He noticed a tax collector ... He knew their thoughts ... he looked round at them all ...' The Beatitudes begin with him 'fixing his eyes on his disciples' before he begins to speak. Throughout the Sermon on the Mount there runs a theme of forgetting one's own needs and desires – leaving these aside, *losing one's life*, giving without any 'hope of return', focusing on what others need rather than on one's own desires. Forgetting oneself, in fact. And when a person manages to forget themselves, and think of others, the person generally stops being shy.

I can hardly imagine any more disastrous exercise for a shy adolescent than practising conversations in front of a mirror, but, amazingly, this is what some psychologists advise. What teenager would not become transfixed with horror simply staring at every pimple, every imperfection? There can be nothing more miserably mesmerizing for a shy person than the sight of one's own reflection opening and shutting its mouth in an attempt to parrot some witty 'conversation opener' or 'chat-up line' gleaned from a self-help manual.

But encourage a shy child to sit down and think about what others are thinking . . . that's a different story.

Suppose you have a child who feels that all the cool kids in her class reject her. (And suppose you *don't* have a child who feels all the cool kids reject her . . . then you really do have problems.) Let her, one afternoon after school, imagine she's an angel flying round her classroom. The angel can see the lives of all the kids in the classroom. How much does your child know about those children, their families, their homes, their favourite games, movies, sports and TV programmes? Gradually let your child see where the gaps in her knowledge are . . . and suggest that it's up to her to fill those gaps, to find out about those children, before she gives up any hope of being their friend.

'If you don't show any interest in them, why should they show any interest in you?' said one mother to her wallflower daughter. 'But they don't want me to play with them,' she wailed for the hundredth time. 'I'm not asking you to play with them as a group,' said the mother. 'Just to take an interest in them as individuals . . . one at a time.'

The self-absorption of the normal growing child makes it very unlikely that she will have thought of asking her classmates questions about their lives. It's a new idea for her. Children are naturally curious, yet can also be remarkably incurious. Asking what may seem like 'nosy' questions might be too much of a challenge − so suggest she does it just once, not perhaps with one of the scary 'cool' kids but with someone a bit more like herself . . . someone else in the class who is a bit shy and reserved. One day on the bus home, let her ask this other child, 'So what will you be doing at the weekend? Got anything planned?' and see what happens.

Who knows, she may soon discover that in fact the other 'shy, reserved' child has a powerful imagination, can think up wonderful make-believe games and makes a great playmate. They may accidentally discover a mutual passion. The chances are, your 'shy' child will suddenly have a new friend and she will have found that new friend all by herself: what could be more confidence-boosting than that?

What your child learns to do in this situation is to put on a mask. She does not feel very curious about the other child's life but because she knows she *should* feel more curious, she puts on a mask and pretends to be curious.

Children need masks in all kinds of situations, none more so than at school. The bullied child above all needs a mask of imperturbability so that the bullies get bored of failing to get a reaction. The angry child needs a mask of calm to prevent his anger from getting him into trouble.

But what about the sad or even depressed child? Masks with smiles on them are undoubtedly the scariest of all masks. It does not feel right, to me, to tell a sad child to 'pull herself together', 'put a brave face on things', 'cheer up'. I would much rather have a quiet space and time to listen to the child talking about her sadness first, asking her how she feels and asking her questions which she can't answer with a yes or a no. I would rather sit by her while she cries herself to sleep than brush off her worries with 'worse things happen at sea'.

Yet after the quiet space and time together sharing the sadness, it cannot do any harm to encourage the child to try putting on a smile . . . just to see if it makes them feel better.

A smile can and does make you feel better. Go into any church which celebrates Eucharist and look out for the bit of the rite called the 'sign of peace'. This is the point at which members of the congregation are meant to turn round and shake hands with each other, saying 'peace be with you'. It takes an exceptionally grumpy person not to assume an immediate smile on saying these words, whatever their facial expression may have been five seconds earlier.

When we do this in our church I always feel as though my head has exploded. I've been lost in the Mass for minutes on end, moving deeper and deeper into my private place, and then, suddenly, I am shaking hands with someone and smiling at them. I can feel my heart beat a bit faster, the adrenalin pumping a bit and the smile seems to burst into my head like a firework. It is a beautiful moment when the sour-faced woman in the row in front of you suddenly turns round and reveals that underneath her apparent sourness is a sweet smile and a warm handshake.

Try it yourself and see the physical effect: your face feels so much more relaxed, and this has a knock-on effect emotionally as you feel more tranquil, more joyous. Yes, you – and the sour-faced woman in front – may have assumed a mask for a moment; that smile may not have reflected your inner thoughts absolutely accurately. You may even have been thinking quite uncharitable things about the sour-faced woman in front. But force yourself to smile and to say those words, 'Peace be with you', and it is as though the unwilling, sour-faced spirit is suddenly seized by the hand, dragged into the sunshine and made to burst out laughing.

Putting on the mask is not always an act of deception; it can be an act of self-encouragement – telling ourselves to become what we would be.

Talents

11

> As for this good-for-nothing servant, throw him into the darkness outside, where there will be weeping and grinding of teeth.
>
> *Matthew 25.14–30*

Several of Jesus' stories feature money. The story of the talents – valuable sums of money which a master gave his servants to look after – is the most uncomfortable of them.

The cruelty of the final words, with the awful image of people being cast into outer darkness for eternity amid wailing and gnashing of teeth (as the King James Bible prefers to express the 'weeping and grinding of teeth' of the New Jerusalem Bible translation quoted here), seems at odds with the 'gentle Jesus meek and mild' of childhood and Sunday school memory.

The story tells of three servants who are entrusted with large sums of money by their master. Two invest the money and make a sizeable profit, the third buries the money – a 'talent' – in the earth, and is afraid to do anything with it. When the master returns, the two who made a profit are praised and rewarded, the third is punished by having his talent taken away and given to the man who has ten already. The third servant's outlook is very bleak indeed.

It seems so unfair! The poor third servant was afraid to lose money by risking it, so he hid it in the ground. He did not do any harm with it, whereas we do not know what exploitation may have been wreaked by the actions of the other two in their pursuit of a fast buck. Why should the poor third servant be cast into outer darkness simply for letting well alone? Socialist Christians in particular, and those who are opposed to anything which smacks of capitalism, profit or usury, have difficulties with this parable as Jesus appears to be praising the profit-makers. And over on the other side of the political arena, the advocates of capitalism sometimes like to seize on this parable as evidence that Christ was a free-market economy enthusiast.

Both attitudes fall into the 'literalist' error made by people of all religions – the error of taking a passage, or sometimes even a few words, from a revered or holy book and trying to apply them to situations that were not even dreamed of by Christ's contemporaries, without regard often for the context in which the passage occurs.

The man with only one talent was not at all badly off – a fact that may be overlooked by both sides of the argument. One talent was a very large sum of money indeed. It has been estimated that it could take a workman such as Joseph, Jesus' father, as much as fifteen years to earn as much as one talent. This is not pocket money, but a sizeable windfall! Such a sum, invested, charitably and wisely, could reap huge dividends and benefit society as a result. The value of a single talent for Jesus' audience must be very significant in the context of this parable – everyone listening to the parable knew how much a talent was worth.

So they knew that there could be no such thing as a *small* talent, no such thing as a talent so *insignificant* that it could be hidden in the ground and forgotten about.

We have learned to be wary of the words 'talent show', especially when combined with the words 'reality TV'. In the twenty-first century our television programme makers have raised the old format of the talent show to an unsurpassed level with shows such as *Pop Idol*, *The X Factor* and a constant stream of similar shows – contests to search for stars of West End musicals, contests for actors and cricket players learning ballroom dancing . . . every year a new twist on the format is devised. What does not change is the concept of using 'ordinary' people (namely, people who do not expect to be paid appearance and repeat fees in the way that professional performers do) to boost TV ratings.

Encouraged to identify with – and just as often, to laugh at – the aspiring amateur performers, audiences watch the show week after week. In a carefully contrived knockout system whereby contestants are slowly whittled down to one winner, the public is invited to identify with contestants and vote for or against them.

It is fashionable to despise the talent shows. But what is wrong – apart from the noise they make – with people with no musical training having a go at singing? The parable of the talents is not about simply making the most of what gifts we have: it is about being prepared to *take risks* with them, to risk making a fool of oneself.

The third servant's mistake was to let the talent sit doing nothing in the ground because he was afraid to take a risk. Reality TV talent shows may be exploitative and cheap, but they at least celebrate people who are not afraid of failure. The self-publicists who take part in these shows are loved by the public who recognize in them the virtue of being determined not to hide their single talent in the ground for fear of exposing it to ridicule.

Risking ridicule and failure is crucial to human endeavour – and at the same time completely against our natures. God often invites us to do something which we fear we can't do, which we fear is beyond our abilities. We cannot quite believe we are 'that' good, even when experience has already suggested that we really are 'that' good. The hugely popular twentieth-century British screen actor David Niven once said that he lived in constant dread of 'being found out'. Even if they have worked hard to get their success, many successful people will, if asked, still admit to the sneaking feeling they 'don't deserve' what they have won. It seems we never quite lose that sense of dread of having our poor little talents exposed to view.

God does not promise success when he invites us to invest our gold coins – in other words, to risk our talents. Taking a risk with a gift means courting disaster, humiliation and even the loss of the gift itself. Father Roger Schutz, founder of the ecumenical Taizé community in France, who died when stabbed to death in front of his congregation in 2005, said: 'At Taizé's beginning when I was alone, I used to say: it's important to take risks, to risk your life perhaps.' Jesus might have framed the story of the talents so that the luckless third servant invested his talent and lost his shirt. But he did not – he told a different story, one which celebrated successful risk-taking.

As adults we generally think of our own talents as being feeble and small, yet we celebrate and praise our children's creations.

Those hesitant attempts to play the recorder; those splodges of paint that might be a house; that curious object that might or might not be a clay pot. But as time goes by, do we continue to celebrate and encourage talents? Do we look for the talents in them, and keep open minds about what they might be?

In the award-winning British feature film *Billy Elliot*, about a boy from a working-class mining family who has a talent for ballet, screenwriter Lee Hall created a powerful tension between the boy's dreams and his father's rigid notions of appropriate male jobs and behaviour. The father in the story is one of the miners involved in the national coal-miners' strike of 1984 over proposed closures of uneconomic pits; he and his elder son are daily taking part in pickets and demonstrations. The younger son, aged 11, secretly takes ballet lessons.

According to the values of this particular community, a son's role is to support what his father thinks and does, more or less unquestioningly, or else be scorned as a 'pansy', even disowned as a traitor. The boy's father, a die-hard trade union man, has to pass through a shattering change of heart when he sees his son's talent with his own eyes. Realizing for the first time that the boy's future is a bigger thing than his own standing with his fellow-strikers, and realizing that money must be raised to further the boy's future as a dancer, he even makes the ultimate act of parental sacrifice and 'self-losing': he signs on with the 'scabs' – the blackleg (strike-breaking) labour – who continue to work at the mine.

His re-education is complete when a ballet grandee informs him that the school expects parents to be 'one hundred per cent behind' their child. From the almost medieval standpoint of the old British working class, where sons support fathers, he has been forced to move to the modern middle-class standpoint of ambition and growth: fathers, it is explained to him, are there to support their children and to raise them up, not the other way around.

Talent shows endorse a very narrow concept of talent. Singing, dancing and acting are celebrated: any kid who is good at sports is celebrated; any artistic aptitude is usually labelled 'talent'. But as the story of the talents shows, there is no such thing as a *small* talent. Every talent is a gold coin of great worth.

So what about the ordinary talents, the ones which are possessed by the vast majority of the population? How many talents in our young people do we, as a society, ignore and bury in the ground?

Let us take a simple example. Almost all young people are born with a natural aptitude for learning a foreign language. It is far easier to learn a foreign language before the age of 18 than afterwards, yet our state education system has allowed the learning of languages to dwindle, by removing it from the National Curriculum after the age of 14.

And what about the remarkable aptitude small children have for learning things off by heart? Most children have an innate ability to learn enough poetry to fill an anthology by the time they leave school. Learning by heart trains the brain and improves the memory. Adults struggle to remember lines but young children's clean, bright, little minds can store them with ease. Yet the practice of learning anything 'by rote' fell into disuse in our schools in the late twentieth century.

And what about the skills that do not feature in talent shows? Bricklaying? Painting and decorating? Accountancy? Surgery? Midwifery? What about skills such as carpentry, which Joseph taught Jesus? These are talents, and they deserve celebration. But only with encouragement from the adults around them will young people be able to take pride in learning, in studying, in developing the talents that never feature on TV talent shows.

The man with one talent probably would not have made so much money from it as the men with three and five talents, but this was not an excuse that the master was prepared to accept. The most important point for parents to take away from this story is this: the size of the talent, or rather the number of talents entrusted, made no difference to the size of the responsibility to put the gift to good use.

It takes courage to invest those gold coins – to risk failure by exposing one's talents to scrutiny, and courage was what the luckless third servant lacked. It is so much easier – but ultimately so much sadder – to spend a life dreaming of what you might have been, rather than to risk a little disappointment by finding out your limitations ... which may, after all, not be as limiting as you had feared.

A kaleidoscope 12

In my Father's house are many mansions ...

John 14.2

When my children were smaller, there were always a few old-fashioned toys in their Christmas stockings, toys which either I or their grandmothers had seen in some gift shop and pounced on as 'charming'. What the children really wanted to find in their stockings, of course, were PlayStations, Gameboys and portable television sets; what they got were whistles, tops, drums and other quaint throwbacks to the time of non-electronic games which appealed to their tasteful but doubtless profoundly annoying parents and grandparents.

Most retro-style toys hold the interest of their new owners for five minutes, at most, if the new owners are aged over three (and if they are aged under three, then European Union regulations insist that they be not given anything interesting to play with because of 'small parts danger').

The retro toys didn't last very long ... except for the kaleidoscopes: cardboard tubes containing cunningly arranged mirrors and − sometimes − handfuls of beads or plastic sparkles. These would hang around the house for months, being casually picked up and played with for a moment not only by children but adults too, before finally meeting their end under an accidental foot. Every time you look through a kaleidoscope, the view changes, and you gaze at it for a while, wondering at its beauty.

I have put a kaleidoscope into the Christian parent's toolkit to remind me that I cannot predict how my children will turn out and that every time I look at them I see new things. I cannot pre-set their qualities and virtues and I cannot expect them to be carbon copies of me. With each turn of the tube, they change and shift and present new and surprising aspects of themselves. Each turn of the tube shakes up the beads inside, and presents a new picture. I can give them some good ideas for making the best of what they are born with but I cannot alter what they have.

A short while ago I thought I might have accidentally become pregnant one night due to a miscalculation of my body clock. Pregnant at 48, with four children already, struggling to get a new career started as a birth educator and hypnotherapist. Pregnant, chained to the drudgery of broken nights and 24-hour watch-fulness – just as we had been thinking that our 'fifties', just around the corner, had signs of developing into rather a pleasant decade. Just as I thought I could start to pursue my own interests as teenagers left the home one by one to find their own lives and stand on their own feet, I was going to be starting right back at the beginning again.

I howled and howled with rage, I cursed my faith, cursed my husband's faith and everything it stood for. 'If you weren't a bloody Catholic,' I screamed at him, 'I wouldn't have become a Catholic and then I wouldn't have these damned scruples, and I'd be able to go off tomorrow morning and get one of those morning-after pills and it would all be done. As it is I can't because obviously that's taking a human life. So now my life is over.'

When the sun rose, I knew I had no choice because my faith had boxed me in. I glumly but resignedly stayed away from the chemist and instead walked around the house with a tape measure, measuring up rooms and wondering if we could somehow turn the home office into another bedroom yet still continue earning our livings as freelances. And when it turned out I was not pregnant after all (it would have been pretty unlikely at 48) I realized that had I gone down to the chemist's and taken the morning-after pill, I would never have known for sure if I had taken a baby's life or not.

It is now legal in the UK for parents who have a very ill child to choose which of their own embryos – fertilized eggs – they can have implanted in the womb, in order to make sure that their next child can be used as a tissue match or blood donor for the older child. This is what is meant by 'designer babies' in the current debate – specifically choosing embryos for strictly medical reasons. However, the procedure has produced much concern because of the possibilities of being allowed to choose children for other characteristics.

Scientists quibble about whether or not an embryo selected from a group can properly be called a 'designer' baby, when its genetic structure has occurred naturally. But such quibbles ignore what makes people feel queasy about the whole process – which is this thought: when I select one child among those I have created – even if they are only eight days from conception – I still have to throw the rejected ones away. And they are my children, too.

Speaking in a BBC documentary about designer babies, a mother who had recourse to this technology because of her constant miscarrying described how 'You phone every day and you're told how they're getting on. I mean it's like having children in nursery; you know, you're told every day how they're progressing through.'[1]

You can see what she means ... but the documentary never invited her to develop this point to its logical end. For when we send our children off to nursery or school, and ring to check on their progress, we do not do so with the intention of putting most of them to death if they do not do well enough. The throwing away of embryos who fail to pass their first exam is something no parent wants to do and it is a decision which causes much anguish, but more and more parents are getting used to the idea.

In the 1982 film *Sophie's Choice* (based on the William Styron novel) the heroine, upon arriving at Auschwitz, is forced by a Nazi officer to choose which of her two children will be allowed to live. It is a hideous idea – to have to choose which of one's children may live or die. It is a request that could only be thought up by a truly sick and perverted mind; yet wind back the years to the point before the child is born, to the days soon after conception, and suddenly Sophie's Choice becomes socially acceptable, even though only the parents who have to make it can tell us how painful it is.

Even if many people accept the idea of picking and choosing embryos for the gravest of medical reasons, the idea of designer babies whose life depends on having the preferred hair or eye colour, or on whether or not he or she will inherit Aunt Mary's intellect or Uncle Stanley's nose, revolts nearly all of us. We instinctively are aware that children come not from a mail-order firm, customized to our specifications. We know that children are sent to us as they are, not as we plan them to be.

When we create a child we shake the kaleidoscope. Once we shake a kaleidoscope we automatically hold it up to the light, to look at the pattern that has been made and admire it for itself. We do not have some kind of plan for what the pattern will look like.

Yet the temptation to judge our children against what we had hoped – no, let's be honest, *planned* them to be – starts right back before conception, when our dreams of glorious parenthood take shape, and carries on into the distant future. Overhearing the elderly mother of a distinguished politician, whom she had raised in a council flat, saying of her son, 'Poor G., I don't think he'll ever be more than a *junior* minister,' was enough to make me realize that this temptation never goes away at all.

We fret continually about whether our child is performing according to certain targets. Is your baby sleeping through the night yet? Is your toddler talking or potty trained or eating independently? None of these pieces of information are to my knowledge yet required on any job application form. We fret about whether they will be the best in school, or the most popular, or the prettiest, instead of admiring what they are.

Some parents find it unbelievably hard to relinquish the setting of an agenda. They start by mapping out every minute of their child's life with activities and opportunities chosen by the parent, not by the child. Very often we are imposing our own childhoods – or the childhoods we would have liked – on to our child: 'I used to adore tennis as a boy – so my son must become a good tennis player.' 'I would have loved to act – so my shy daughter must go to weekend stage school.'

Academic success, a highly paid career, beauty, sporting success and popularity – we long for all of these for our children, perhaps failing to see that for this particular child these might not all be achievable – or even all that important.

We often read of the fall in priestly vocations: few young people want to take holy orders now. I think this is only partly due to a decline in belief; it is also due to the widening range of other ways of expressing the desire to 'do good' – such as by working for a charity. And it is also due to the pressure of parental expectations. Parents who declare that they 'would not want to pressurize their son/daughter' to take holy orders may at the same time be subtly pressurizing the son or daughter to slot meekly into the rat race, just like mum and dad: 'do what you like, son, as long as you are as materialist and money-obsessed as us . . .'

Fixed and immobile ambitions for our children have been compared rightly[2] to the 'false idols' of Ezekiel 14.4: 'Son of man, these men have enshrined their foul idols in their hearts and placed the cause of their sinning right before their eyes.' We do not necessarily think of exam success, for example, as a false idol; rather, it is something to be sought, chased after, celebrated. Yet if we allow this ambition to stand 'right before our eyes', blocking a clear view of our child, it has become a false idol.

Human beings are kaleidoscopes: ever-changing combinations of broken pieces that suddenly amaze by their beauty . . . and are best when held up carefully, lovingly, so that the view of them is not blocked by our fixed ideas about what they ought to be like; but so that the light shines through them.

Notes

1. *Horizon: Who's Afraid of Designer Babies?*, BBC television programme.
2. Paul David Tripp, *Age of Opportunity*, (Phillipsburg, NJ: P&R Publishing 1997).

Fireside faith 13

But when you pray, go to your private room, shut yourself in,
and so pray to your Father who is in that secret place.

Matthew 6.6

Bernard always had a few prayers in the hall and some whiskey
afterwards as he was rather pious but Mr Salteena was not very
adicted to prayers so he marched up to bed.

Daisy Ashford, The Young Visiters

Nearly five million people in the United Kingdom go to a
Christian church of some sort or other, on a weekly basis.[1] I call
that a sizeable minority, in a country of 60.2 million people, far
larger than you would think judging by the media silence on what
goes on inside churches. What it does not tell us is how many of
those people manage to bring their faith back home with them.

This chapter is about breaking through the invisible glass wall
we often erect across the threshold; the barrier we impose which
stops us from talking about our faith the minute we are outside
church. Yet if we don't bring faith to 'that secret place' we call
home, it is not really faith at all.

Embarrassment is the main enemy. No self-respecting British
man feels anything but silly praying with his children, at first. Most
of the families I have spoken to who can get past the embarrassment factor start off with a bedtime prayer, preferably when the
child is very small, and allow this to 'grow' into a more complete,
thoughtful ritual and an opportunity to say 'sorry' if there has been
a conflict.

Sneaking faith into the average British home is very like
sneaking greens into children's food. You have to hide it at first,
then you gradually get bolder, progressing from a sauce in which
the healthy stuff has been mushed into an unrecognizable purée

that could easily be tomato ketchup, towards one where carrots, broccoli and mushrooms can hold their heads up courageously, no longer skulking in an amorphous mass but now truly 'proud to be veg'.

Bedtime stories, for example, can include a range of well-told, illustrated Bible stories from bright and varied picture books, as well as the usual secular stories. Let them sit about on the shelves with the other books. Many Catholic families have crosses, crucifixes and religious images up on walls around the house . . . along with all the other pictures. Even a picture of a church helps bring faith into the home, in a tiny way. When you are out, pointing out churches in the landscape around you underlines how Christianity has shaped our geography.

Have a Bible somewhere where you can find it in a hurry; explore the world of prayer books, some of which are lovely – though others are desperate. Keep devotional books where children can get at them . . . especially, when they are a little bored and have nothing else to do, so are more likely to be tempted to open them up. Avoid anything clad in white tooled leather, and not only on grounds of taste: faith books are for reading with a cup of cocoa, thumbing through with fingers still damp from the washing-up, and for referring to frequently, not for calcifying into 'presentation editions' that gather dust. When you start praying with your children you may find that a set formula, a prayer you have found in a book or which the child has learned at school or Sunday school, is most comfortable. But why not let your child lead the way by throwing in her own bits and pieces? Try to steer her away from prayers for material goods and stress that it is not for us to tell God *how* to answer our prayers. Besides, he quite often answers not simply with 'Yes', but with 'No', 'Later' and even 'No, you do it, you lazy so-and-so . . .' Focus more on celebrating what we have been given, rather than asking for things; on being sorry for what we have done ourselves, rather than on feeling sorry for ourselves.

Children are surprisingly good at talking aloud to God: better than most of us adults. If your child's freestyle 'bits and pieces' praying opens up thoughts about friendship problems, about caring for people in the family, about wondering about sick relatives and whether they will get better, then go with the flow. Try not to let your embarrassment show: relax, and enjoy it.

Let children learn formulas because these give them a framework to work with ... but also encourage them to build on the formula with their own language, or suggest more adult turns of phrase yourself.

A prayer that is a complete, total, end-of-day prayer is made up of four parts which can be remembered by the acronym ACTS:

> **A**doration: the acknowledgement that God is infinitely big whereas I am finite, and small.
>
> **C**onfession: sincere acknowledgement of what I have done wrong; feelings of repentance.
>
> **T**hanks: thinking about what we have got and can be grateful for.
>
> **S**upplication: asking God for support and strength or for someone we are thinking of.

Prayer is a learned experience like dieting or giving up smoking; we rarely get it right first time. It needs practice, just like dieting and giving up smoking. One attempt at prayer is not enough, as King Claudius discovered in *Hamlet* when he tried praying after murdering Hamlet's father. I think a lot of families feel prayer is nice to teach children to do, but not something for grown-ups to do: with an attitude like that, how can they expect to pass on faith? If you never see your parents pray, why should you do it yourself?

Although it is a *learned* thing, prayer should not be *automatic* (like changing gear when driving). Prayer is harder to learn than driving, because it requires constant vigilance. Nor should the words become a 'magic spell' or 'babbling' (Matthew 6.7).

On the other hand, routine prayers said rhythmically and with the ease of familiarity have been shown to be good for you: they provide the emotional anchors we need through the day. The embarrassment factor soon melts away as your own faith becomes firmer. Most of us do not progress beyond a rather babyish, Sunday school level of theology, and are never aware of any grown-up writing on faith. It is hardly surprising: the media silence on faith books, particularly on books written by Christians as opposed to militant atheists, is deafening. Even quality broadsheet newspapers send out only a tiny handful of devotional or religious books to their book review team for inclusion in the books section. Books attacking religion, yes, you will find plenty of these: books written by believers explaining their religion, almost never. So unless you scout around a bit, and ask your pastor or priest, you will not get to hear about books that can move your understanding of this complex and sometimes difficult faith forwards beyond the nursery. Yet there are plenty out there.

Another barrier to bringing faith 'indoors', perhaps a more serious one, is a sense of unworthiness. I hate saying Grace at table when there has just been a family row because, to be frank, it makes me feel hypocritical and scummy. It feels more honest just to hunch my shoulders and sulk. However hard I try to put the mask on, praying does not seem 'appropriate'. Yet these are, in fact, the most appropriate times for prayer – prayer helps to calm us down and helps us to let our love for each other flow freely. Prayer is not a special occasion thing.

Saying Grace at mealtimes is another 'way in' to getting past the glass wall that stops families bringing their church life home. Choose one which you like, but choose neither a joke Grace (such as 'Rubadubdub, thanks for the grub') nor something in Latin (unless your family are all fluent classicists), and stick with it, even in public places. (The other people in the restaurant are thinking about their own meals, not about you . . . honest!)

After you have got used to bedtime prayers and Grace at meals, you have the beginnings of a framework for praying, which gives your children a real spiritual advantage over the rest of the world. Your children will not be struggling to 'find their spirituality' in later life, because they have grown up knowing all along where to find it. Your children will not be seizing on bits and pieces of half-digested faiths for 'spiritual enlightenment' because they will have already experienced a spiritual home.

And once you have experienced the ultimate embarrassment threshold – saying Grace in a motorway service station restaurant – you may be emboldened to look for more 'prayable moments'. What about praying together before the kids set off for school? Or on the first day of term? What about offering up thanks for a sunny day, for a successful school report, for getting the cat back safely from the visit to the vet?

When we think of bringing faith back home – making home a holy place, if you like – in one sense we are talking about something that has already taken place, because our homes are automatically the centre of our lives, and as soon as faith is at the centre of our lives as well then the two simply gel together.

Making home a holy place does not mean turning it into some kind of New Age meditation centre. Family life is inevitably full of tensions, because family relationships matter so much to us, particularly when seen in comparison to relationships with people at work, friends and acquaintances. A family row is always a *big* row, because it is always more significant than a quarrel anywhere else. There is always so much more at stake – our love. No wonder the workplace often seems like a calm, relaxed haven in comparison to home.

We should feel free to acknowledge the holiness of family life by allowing prayer into it. By allowing prayer in, we open our eyes to the truth that family life is a fount of holiness – because it is about people we love, and God is love. Family life is made up of love, and so much is risked within its conflicts and struggles – in love we risk our hearts and our happiness, no less. So before we even begin to pray, family life is already a sacred thing, and the home is already a sacred place; praying within it is simply the right thing to do.

Note

1. 'Churchgoing in the UK', survey by Tearfund, 2007.

Ears

14

'He that hath ears to hear, let him hear.'

Matthew 11.15, AV

'Anyone who has ears for listening should listen.'

Luke 14.35

There are eight (on my count) separate instances in the Gospels of Jesus using these words to top-and-tail his utterances. They are such familiar words, so reminiscent of a fairytale opening, that it does not take much familiarity with the Bible to bring us to the point where we almost stop 'hearing' them. We all have ears to hear, unless we are physically deaf. Jesus is making a joke: if you cannot hear what he has said, then you cannot have ears to hear . . . it is a joke not too distantly related to the old chestnut about the lecturer who says, 'If you can't hear me at the back, please raise your hands.'

Jesus is saying that we all have the ability to hear what he has to tell us. It is up to us how much we do to process the words: how much we allow them to sink in; whether we wish to be like the stony ground in the parable of the sower, or the rich and fertile ground.

Listening is a vital parental skill, as new mothers quickly find when they give birth in hospital. A mother who is sharing a postnatal ward with several other mothers and their babies is often struck by how easily she can pick out the cry of her own baby from the others, even though she has not heard it for more than a few minutes. She instinctively tunes into the precise timbre of her baby's voice, when anyone else would find it impossible to tell one baby's cry from another. This perceptiveness is a wonderful gift, worth treasuring and nurturing; fortunately, the barbaric practice of separating new mothers from their babies by placing the babies in hospital nurseries has died out in the UK, so our new mums have more chance to bond with their babies and recognize that early little voice, the only tool a baby has to tell his mother something is not right.

The Hindu god Ganesha has elephant ears to enable him the more easily to hear the needs of his people. Listening is what helps us to hear the needs of our children. If we study good parenting technique or read good books on the subject,[1] we quickly find out how to listen to our children's needs, how to 'hear' the emotion or the problem that lies behind the words that they say.

The technique is very simple: next time your child comes to you with a story about something that happened at school, just let them talk and let them know you are listening carefully. Keep your reactions under wraps initially: listen before you judge what your reaction should be. Let the whole story come out, in the child's own words.

The next step is to let the child go back over his or her own feelings about the story. Small children may find it comforting to have a name put to their feelings: 'That sounds as though it was frustrating.' 'It sounds as though that made you feel left out.' 'That must have made you feel happy/proud/angry/lonely/confused.'

Where a child brings you a problem to solve, turn the problem back to the child: 'What do you think is the fairest way to sort out who's going to be team captain?' 'Can you think of a way of doing the school project which you and your friend would both feel happy with?' Help a little only if the child is really stuck ... and give them time to think about it on their own first.

By listening to children before jumping in with what WE have to say – our soothing noises, our interpretations, our exclamations of shock and astonishment – we will invariably hear a lot more of the story than we would have otherwise. So let those parents who have ears to hear, hear.

Another use for those ears is for listening to advice. Virtually from the moment it becomes known that we are expecting a baby, parents receive a great deal of advice from other people. Advice from TV experts, from magazines, from websites. Advice from friends, relatives, workmates, bosses, customers, shopkeepers, even occasionally doctors and health visitors are allowed to get a word in edgeways.

There is a big industry in parenting advice; and everybody thinks they are an expert. A client of mine once walked into a business meeting when six months pregnant, and immediately received 20 minutes' advice from the man next to her – a complete stranger – on how to handle her labour and the birth of her child.

And the worst thing about advice is that half of it generally conflicts with the other half. The ideal pair of parent's ears would not only be ultra-sensitive and able to hear the sound of the parent's own baby crying at long distance (now that *would* be useful) but also would have an automatic filter system that filters out bad advice from good ... as soon as it has been heard, rather than six months later after the poor parent has acted on it and found it to be worse than useless.

Let us look at some of the advice parents have been given over the years.

Here is Dr J. B. Watson, a US psychologist writing in 1928:

> Nearly all of us have suffered from over-coddling in our infancy. How does it show? It shows in invalidism ... coddling is a dangerous experiment ... the fact that our children are always crying and always whining shows the unhappy, unwholesome state they are in. There is a sensible way of treating children. Treat them as though they were young adults. Never hug and kiss them, never let them sit on your lap. If you must, kiss them once on the forehead when they say good night. Shake hands with them in the morning ... try it out. In a week's time you will be utterly ashamed of the mawkish, sentimental way you have been handling it ...'

Similarly, Dr Frederick Truby-King, a New Zealand psychologist whose theory of strict infant feeding was very popular in the UK and the USA during the 1920s and 1930s, advised mothers to feed their newborn babies every four hours and never at night; to scrub their nipples to 'harden' them before breastfeeding and not to play with their babies in case it 'excited' them. Truby-King was completely ignorant of the physiology of breastfeeding; of how breast milk cannot be supplied unless stimulated by the baby's sucking, of how this cannot happen unless the baby indicates when he/she is hungry; of how a newborn baby's stomach is the size of a hazelnut and can hold only a little milk at a time. The irony of the Truby-King method is that he seriously thought he was *promoting* breastfeeding, whereas in fact he created an entire mythology around it, giving generations and generations of Western women the idea that breastfeeding – something their bodies were built to do – is 'difficult'.

These doctors were reflecting what seemed right at the time. They were advising certain parenting methods because they sincerely believed them to be correct. It is a matter of speculation whether they thought these methods were correct because of the society they lived in – a society devastated by one war, and constantly in fear of more war – or the particular way in which their generation interpreted Christian values. Whatever lay behind such advice, we do not approve of it nowadays. But what will future generations think of the advice given to parents today?

Will the obsession with boosting children's self-esteem one day be discredited as pointless? Will the strictly controlled negotiations of experts such as Jo Frost, TV's Supernanny and queen of the 'naughty step', be criticized as cruel and rigid?

It is always instructive to look at advice from the point of seeing how it aids not the receiver of the advice, but the giver – or, in the case of parenting advice, the society in which the children are to grow up. It is worth looking at the circumstances from which the advice comes before judging it to be universally useful.

We are in a very prosperous society, but one with high material values. In the UK, property values combine with women's career expectations to turn the two-income family into an almost universal norm, and certainly something to which one-income or no-income families are encouraged to aspire. The voluntary stay-at-home mother has been subtly replaced by the trophy 'yummy mummy', a living indication of her husband's high earning power – he is so rich that she does not *need* to go out to work, you see. Ordinary stay-at-home mums, scrimping and saving to get by on their partner's moderate income, attract very little attention and are on the wane. Most new mothers, when asked in surveys, would like to stay at home with their children until the youngest is five years old. But not many will be able to do so.

At the same time, we have a falling birth rate: fewer children. Our society does not like to have children wandering all over the place taking risks and getting into trouble. It likes children to be somewhere safe and preferably out of sight of the rest of the community, which is not interested in children at all.

Our children have to adapt very quickly to a social setting – the day nursery. They have to adapt to being looked after by different people. They have to learn to be content with being separated from their mother for long hours every day. They have to adapt to an institutional timetable because that makes it easier for their parents and carers to plan ahead. They have to learn to get on with other children, so that they can be left with them without all hell breaking loose.

Most parenting advice currently in favour is adapted to the needs of this society just as cunningly, though I hope not as cruelly, as the advice of Drs Watson and Truby-King was adapted to the society of their day. Most parenting advice focuses on having children accept the existence of a 'workplace' – the nursery – alongside the existence of home, almost from birth.

Much parenting advice seems to me to be training children to enter the workplace by treating their entire world as a kind of corporate headquarters. It focuses on encouraging children to negotiate with each other; but not to explore the neighbourhood on their bikes. It focuses on obeying in-house rules and playing nicely with each other; but not on using their own resources to play on their own. Creativity is celebrated, but not helping with the housework, or messing about by the river until sunset.

I do not criticize the parenting advice of today; I am simply pointing out that it is serving the needs of the society in which it belongs.

Advice that benefits the giver more than the receiver is usually best avoided. So too is advice that saves the giver a bit of guilt: especially advice given in the form of a newspaper column written by a journalist whose sole claim to expertise is having had children. Much of this opinionated advice is written to absolve the writer of any guilt for any decisions she or he may have made in the past, decisions that were, in the cold light of day, rather iffy.

So, women who give birth without drugs are categorized as

'earth mothers who get behind a bush and squat'[2] by a columnist who had an elective caesarean for non-medical reasons. Women who breastfeed are scorned as 'bovine' and 'zealots'[3] by a columnist who did not. Mothers who stay at home with their children receive the most criticism: they are regularly mocked and reviled as 'mothers superior' who show up their working 'sisters'[4] . . . usually by women who earn a lot of money.

Advice which saves the advice-giver some trouble is usually not the best advice. Advice that prevents the receiver from achieving an outcome a bit different, and possibly better, than that achieved by the giver is not usually the best advice.

A mother, particularly a highly educated mother, who chooses to look after her own children at the expense of a career, makes a lonely choice. Her contemporaries from university, who had no truck with 'career breaks' let alone being SAHMs ('stay-at-home mums'), now have gigantic financial-sector salaries, squillion-pound homes and children away at expensive boarding schools. The mother who turned her back on all this in order to be at the school gate every afternoon did not go wrong; she simply chose to use her ears to listen to the voice within her heart, rather than the voice of society's advice-givers.

Notes

1. E.g., the classic *How to Talk so Kids will Listen and Listen so Kids will Talk* by Adele Faber and Elaine Mazlish, first published in 1980 and still one of the best parenting texts ever written!
2. Alice Miles: 'Natural Birth? Hello! This is the 20th Century', *The Times*, London, April 2007.
3. India Knight, 'Stop Breast-Beating, Sisters', *Sunday Times*, London, August 2007.
4. 'Kate calls the stay-at-home women the Mothers Superior and classes herself a Mother Inferior, which is how I personally feel a lot of the time. I don't think working mothers judge the stay-home mothers – they know they've made the big sacrifice to be with their kids – but I think some judging may go on the other way round' (novelist and columnist Allison Pearson, talking about the heroine of her novel *I Don't Know How She Does It* in an interview in bookreporter.com, May 2003).

Hedges, walls and barbed wire fences   15

Anyone who welcomes one little child like this in my name welcomes me. But anyone who is the downfall of one of these little ones who have faith in me would be better drowned in the depths of the sea with a great millstone round his neck.

Matthew 18.5–6

But anyone who is the downfall of one of these little ones who have faith, would be better thrown into the sea with a great millstone hung round his neck.

Mark 9.42

Causes of falling are sure to come, but alas for the one through whom they occur! It would be better for him to be thrown into the sea with a millstone round the neck than to be the downfall of a single one of these little ones.

Luke 17.1–2

There cannot be more confusion about any aspect of what constitutes Christian parenting than there is about the issue of discipline. The first puzzle of all is – why is it, when Christ was so specifically non-violent, that so many so-called Christians believe in hitting children? Using violence of any kind against children, even the 'loving chastisement' beloved of some Christian parenting manuals, is by definition anti-Christian. It is teaching children to be violent. 'Love is always patient and kind,' begins the most famous passage of St Paul, quoted at a thousand wedding ceremonies every weekend. Patience and kindness do not admit of hitting children.

The 'downfall' spoken of in the quotations from the Gospels

above is a roundabout translation of the Greek word *skandalise*, which means 'offend'. Jesus is here talking of actions which cause 'these little ones' – the next generation, the children whom he has gathered around him – to lose their faith, to fall down. And what has been a more certain cause of turning away from the faith than harsh punishments meted out by self-righteous Christian teachers and parents over the centuries?

We all know perfectly well that children need firm moral boundaries – a clear idea of what is right and wrong and a firm purpose in wanting to do right. But there are boundaries – and there are boundaries, as any landscape gardener will tell you.

Suppose you surround your garden with brick walls, which are absolutely immoveable, but against which you can bounce a tennis ball satisfyingly. Brick walls make good boundaries, but the problem with them is that once you have climbed over on to the other side, it is difficult to get back into the garden. They also require continual maintenance.

Or you can grow hedges, which take a lot of time and care to develop. These are more beautiful, more friendly at least to look at. Children and hedges live happily together, except when the children try to bounce balls off them, at which point the ball simply disappears into the hedge – a deeply frustrating experience for the child, who might then long for the comforting solidity of the brick wall.

Lastly, there are barbed wire fences, which are ugly, cruel and which everybody, adults and children alike, stays well away from – because everyone is afraid of getting hurt.

Any harsh punishment-based type of discipline, especially any kind of physical punishment, is the equivalent of the barbed wire fence. It is not the choice of gardeners who want to create something lasting and loveable; it is more the choice of factory farmers keeping cattle in, and raiders out.

You would have thought this kind of disciplinary style had gone completely out of fashion; unfortunately, perhaps as a kind of misguided reaction to the relaxed parenting style which has been popular since the 1970s, punishment-based disciplinary styles enjoyed a vogue among Christian parents in the United States in the 1990s, in the form of books and courses promoted by 'gurus' such as Gary and Anne Ezzo.

Their strict 'biblical' disciplining of babies, enforcing routines for sleeping and feeding from very early on, endorses physical retribution at various levels. They urge parents of newborn babies not to let their children 'manipulate' them – 'manipulation' being their view of natural demand feeding or attachment parenting.

The cornerstone of their babycare advice is 'Parent-directed feeding'. This involves scheduled feeds and mothers are advised to leave their babies to cry until the time for the next feed arrives. The system has no basis in the scientifically known nutritional or emotional needs of babies, or the underlying physical and hormonal processes on which successful breastfeeding depends. One of the Ezzos' books cited biblical verses to support their theories of baby feeding: even Jesus' words on the Cross, 'My God, why have you forsaken me?' being dragged in to support their belief that a baby who is crying, but who has been fed and changed recently, should be left alone to cry.

It is only a short step from leaving babies to cry in order to stop them from 'manipulating' parents to treating older children like hardened criminals. The Ezzos endorsed physical punishments such as the following for a ten-month-old baby who smears baby food in his hair: 'squeeze the baby's hand until it hurts enough to make him stop ...'

At this point in the Ezzo child-rearing programme, where the system starts advocating discipline in the highchair, parents who were initially seduced by the system's promises of 'training' a baby to sleep through the night, or by the idea that it would be fine to dump the baby in a playpen and ignore them for 30 minutes twice a day, because that was 'playpen time', probably quietly put the book down and never picked it up again, or tiptoed out of the classroom door, never to return. The Californian church where the Ezzos first developed their system broke off connection with the couple in 2000. However, enough parents seem to have been seduced into buying the system to continue to make it profitable, because it is promoted now by a new company, Parentwise Solutions.

The idea that babies manipulate adults is absurd. When they feel hunger and fear, babies naturally respond by crying, the only alarm system they possess. It is equally obscene to regard a little child who is unconsciously experimenting with the new texture of a foodstuff as 'naughty'.

No home-grown Christian parenting expert has advocated physical punishment in the UK for many years. In the 1980s the Catholic writer Lynette Burrows tried to make a stand for it, with little success. Back in 1976 another American, Dr James Dobson, won some notoriety and became well known in the UK because he advocated spanking as part of discipline, suggesting that parents rationalize it to a child like this: 'When I tell you to stay in the front yard, it's because I don't want you to run in the street and get hit by a car. I love you and I don't want anything to happen to you. If you don't mind me, I'll have to spank you to help you remember how important it is. Do you understand?'[1]

Dobson advocates spanking children from babyhood up to the age of eight. 'It is not necessary to beat the child into submission; a little bit of pain goes a long way for a young child. However, the spanking should be of sufficient magnitude to cause the child to cry genuinely,' he wrote. He warns that the crying should be allowed to continue as long as there are 'genuine tears'. Dobson is not a bad man: he is genuinely concerned about parental smackings that 'get out of hand' resulting in injury or death.

But he also believes that a spanking actually increases closeness between parent and child, writing:

After the emotional ventilation, the child will often want to crumple to the breast of his parent, and he should be welcomed with open, warm, loving arms. At that moment you can talk heart to heart. You can tell him how much you love him, and how important he is to you. You can explain why he was punished and how he can avoid the difficulty next time. This kind of communication is not made possible by other disciplinary measures, including standing the child in the corner or taking away his firetruck.

Now there are many loving and normal parents who have stooped to using violence occasionally, and it is wrong to stigmatize them. I know I used to use violence. I felt it was necessary to get a quick message across and like many other parents I saw 'nothing wrong with the occasional slap'. I used to agree with Lynette Burrows[2] when she stated that smacking a child is 'quick, educative and doesn't waste anyone's time'. I could see that a quick slap may be less trouble all round than a laborious session of putting a furious, hysterical toddler on the naughty step, since it can be followed with a hug and a smile. I was briefly seduced by Dobson's idea that a slap 'helps a child remember' what he is supposed to have done wrong.

But you know what? The whole idea of corporal punishment simply *does not work*. I tried it, and I can report that the smacking *never did any good*. I cannot think of a single occasion when I felt anything but soiled and degraded by doing it. It never improved my children's behaviour at all, whereas consistent non-violent sanctions and the setting of a good example have done.

The hug and the smile following the smacking simply made me feel seedy, ashamed, ingratiating. The emotional closeness that Dr Dobson promised would be the aftermath of 'the parent's demonstration of his authority' certainly never took place for me as a result of smacking any of my children.

A story of one of Dr Dobson's clients, who told how her fifteen-month-old child, after being spanked on the legs with a switch in the Dobson-approved manner, approached her mother for a hug saying 'Love, mommy' is cited by Dr Dobson as evidence of how 'the child will often reveal his affection when the emotion (of being punished) has passed'. The same episode might equally be read as proof of how upsetting and confusing for a tiny child such treatment is. This was not an improvement in emotional closeness: it was a small child trying desperately to regain a closeness which the smacking had destroyed.

Whenever I used violence against a child of mine, I felt a distance opening up between us. The clear effect on my children was to harden their hearts, embittering them with resentment. The point of James Dobson's system seemed to be to shatter the child's confidence in his parent's feelings for him *so badly that he is driven to begging for reassurance that he is still loved*.

Dobson complains that small children 'play games' with parents, running them ragged: yet at the same time, he seems to be advocating that parents play mind games with children which are vastly more unpleasant, since they come from a position of power. The kind of 'emotional closeness' Dr Dobson describes as the aftermath of a smacking is creepy, slightly sexual and has a whiff of sadism that one hopes is entirely unwitting.

Smacking my children did not increase their 'respect' for me: on the contrary, it diminished it. Whatever the Ezzos and Dobsons of this world imagine, smacking a child does not make that child *respect* the parent more: this is a clear case of confusing fear with respect. Any respect my beloved children have for me, I have had to work hard to win back, after the loss of respect which physical violence inevitably brings in its wake.

In short, hitting little children is a mug's game: it has no part in a Christian upbringing.

If you set yourself up as a police officer, you soon become more interested in your arrest record than in your rehabilitation record, always ready to catch children doing wrong, less interested in catching them doing right. If you start off treating your children like criminals, they will behave like criminals. Constant threats of punishment and fear of consequences including physical pain soon erect a high razor-wire fence around the garden of your child's life; and once your child has worked out how to get hold of a pair of wire clippers, you will never see them again.

Parents who have very firm, but rather inflexible rules (but who are not necessarily violent towards their children in any way) I see as another type: the brick-wall parents. Their virtue is that they are warm and solid, and not without humour; they offer excellent security, particularly when children are young. Because they are not easily persuaded, they provide a place from which a young person may launch out in rebellion – a hard surface for children to kick a ball against. It is hard to be a rebel if you have nothing to rebel against.

There are not very many of these parents about these days; and the drawback of being a brick-wall parent is that you can become a bit wall-eyed. Being closed to negotiation over big issues can mean you are closed to negotiation over small issues as well. The brick-wall parents may not know how to cope when their child grows up a bit and commits what are by most people's standards quite minor breaches of 'respect', such as getting a wacky haircut or staying out all night with a boyfriend.

Furthermore, if you belong to a firm faith, then the faith can be the brick wall for both you and your child – your faith, in other words, is what provides the solid and unmoving set of values. You need not feel you have to be an entire moral system all by yourself: some brick-wall parents are not so much garden walls as battlements.

That leaves us with the third of our emblematic forms of boundary: that very British institution, the garden hedge. Luxuriant, natural, organic and yet impenetrable, sometimes frustrating in that nothing bounces off it, but sinks into it; in constant need of attention; the most difficult kind of boundary to look after, but the most beautiful.

The health of the 'garden hedge' depends on your example, your continual attempts to 'model' a Christ-like way of doing things. This is what makes it such a high-maintenance piece of shrubbery.

The effectiveness of the garden hedge depends on the parent's efforts to be consistent – especially in following through with warnings such as 'if you do that again, I am confiscating your Nintendo/PS3/bike/TV for X number of days'. The X in that sentence needs to be thought out carefully – how long can you reasonably confiscate the said item? Are you going to be able to do it effectively or are you going to back out because it is too much trouble? Warn children of consequences, by all means, but be prepared to follow up with delivery.

Hedge parents are honest when they slip up, when they fail to be consistent; they are not afraid to confront their own imperfections. They are not afraid to let their children see them saying sorry or being contrite: if the parent never shows contrition, why should the child bother? Above all, hedge-parenting has lots of room for hugs, forgiveness and laughter.

Hedge-parenting depends on you, the parent, establishing a deep, close relationship with your child and working hard to keep it healthy and vibrant. This is a relationship completely unlike the distant relationship based on fear which is seen in the barbed-wire style of parenting. And unlike the brick-wall style of parenting, it depends on the parent offering the child choices, guiding their choices but also giving them ample space to make decisions for themselves.

Hedge-parenting allows organic growth. The child is involved in the process, drawn in as a willing participant rather than being treated as a criminal who must be corrected and punished. One excellent American Catholic parenting guru, Greg Popcak,[3] is a classic example of a hedge-boundary parent. He stresses warmth, affection and mutual respect, and points out the difference between parents who yell 'problem-focused questions' at their children, and those who instead pose 'solution-focused questions' – questions which look for answers, often from the child himself.

So, faced with, for example, a child who habitually won't do his homework unless screamed at several times, this approach asks, 'what is different about the days when he DOES do his homework without a fight (however rare these days may be), and the days when we have a huge battle? What is special about those times when the right thing happens?'

Likewise, instead of 'How stupid are you?' the hedge parent says to a child who has seriously stepped over the mark, 'I know you are bright. Now how can you use your brain to solve the problem we have here?' And instead of 'Why can't you understand . . .?' the hedge-parent is more likely to open the plea with 'This is what I need from you . . . now, how can I help you to make this happen for us?'

The drawback of hedge-parenting is that it can be messy and time-consuming: it's that problem of the lost tennis ball, you see. Once you commit yourself to answering provoking questions about why we do this and that, once you start opening discussions about right and wrong, then you will soon find yourself searching around in the bottom of the hedge for the lost ball and sometimes you will emerge rather dishevelled. If you had a brick-wall upbringing yourself, or even, Lord forbid, a barbed-wire upbringing, you may find you do not have the tools ready for maintaining a hedge; you will need to do some more homework, some more prayer, to search out the books and teachers of your faith to support you; and then you will begin to learn more about the questions of your own life, and you can search for answers together with your child.

Notes

1. James Dobson, *Dare to Discipline* (Toronto and New York: Bantam Books, 1981, 1970).
2. Lynette Burrows, *Good Children* (Oxford: Butterworth-Heinemann Ltd, 1985); republished in 2002 as *Good Children: A Common-Sense Guide to Bringing up your Child* (Oxford: Family Publications, 2002).
3. Greg Popcak, *Parenting with Grace* (Huntington, IN: Our Sunday Visitor Publications, 2000).

A bin liner – de-clutter your family's life 16

> And he instructed them to take nothing for the journey except a staff – no bread, no haversack, no coppers for their purses. They were to wear sandals but, he added, 'Don't take a spare tunic.'
>
> *Mark 6.8–9*

'Live Simply' was to be the theme of the family retreat. For a week, we were to focus on the concept of de-cluttering our lives, practically but more important spiritually. 'Live Simply' is the slogan of a Catholic Agency for Overseas Development (CAFOD) campaign designed to encourage us to spend a bit more on charity and a bit less on ourselves, so it seemed an excellent idea to build a Catholic Family Week around it.

Catholic People's Weeks (CPW) are a kind of holy Butlins: group holidays organized by a small charity, entirely run by volunteers. We began going to them when our children were in the demanding though immensely enjoyable age range that stretches from three up to eleven. We discovered that various old stagers had been booking themselves into CPW since their own children were small, and were now attending with their grandchildren in tow.

The formula is a winning one, or would be if more people knew about it. The CPW organizers hire a venue – usually a boarding school, since these have plenty of multi-bedded rooms, are child-friendly and available during school holidays – and a motley crew of all-sorts descends on the venue for a week. During the mornings the adults have a rare opportunity to think about some aspect of faith without interruption while a team of trained young volunteers, in another part of the venue, lead the children in activities ranging from basketball to writing an entire play for performance during Mass.

So what exactly will I need to pack to send a family of two adults, two teens and two youngsters off on a seven-day retreat?

Deep breath ... here we go: six bags each containing, on average, six sets of underwear and one spare, four tops and four pairs of jeans, two fleeces or similar, pyjamas and spare shoes: 210 separate items of clothing in all. Six toiletry bags containing toothpaste (we all like different ones), toothbrushes, skincare products (some of us have eczema, some of us just NEED a lot of skincare), shaving gel, razors, enough makeup to allow me and my elder daughter to feel at least minimally pampered (half a dozen items each), five different shampoos – one for blondes, one for brunettes, one for dandruff-sufferers, one for serious dandruff-sufferers and one for the solitary 'normal' person in the family – and of course the conditioners which complement the shampoos, two shower gels (one for men, and one more suitable for ladies), six hairbrushes, six flannels; plus six towels and a hairdryer. That's 63 items, many of them reflecting perhaps excessive determination of various family members to assert their gender role.

Next we pack jewellery and accessories for me – well, the more accessories you take, the fewer outfits you need, right? Five pairs of earrings, three different crosses and a bangle (besides what I was wearing in the car) and three scarves. For my elder daughter: four pairs of earrings, six different Alice bands, five bangles and three scarves – 39 items.

Five different MP3 players, headsets and chargers, a laptop with modem cable and power cable, five mobile phones and their chargers, the speakers for my MP3 player, a digital radio (because the radio in my MP3 player isn't as good as the manufacturers seem to imagine), the power cables for these last two, four DVDs for playing on the computer if things get boring, approximately 23 books: I reckon we are on 59 items here in the 'technology' section.

For the journey: one bag containing six bottles of water, five packets of crisps, five apples, six bananas, a packet of Jacobs Cream Crackers: 23 items. For use once we are on the retreat: six coats, six pairs of Wellington boots or walking boots, a football, a cricket bat, a tennis ball for using as a cricket ball, a pack of cards, some sheet music for the concert evening: 17 items.

That's a total of 411 items. This is our absolute bare minimum. I am not counting, of course, the bags in which these items are kept, nor the contents of my handbag, which has to be replaced annually with a larger and more capacious model because of the amount of stuff I need to cart around with me; nor the contents of my husband's pockets. I have probably grossly underestimated the number of items in my sponge bag, not to mention my daughter's – and of course I have not counted the various illicit Gameboys and other contraband smuggled in by my children.

Living simply sounds beautiful. The very words have a grace and elegance which makes us all sigh with longing. They conjure up a vision of a plainly polished wooden table, a simple flower arrangement or bowl of fruit perhaps catching the rays of the setting sun. One imagines a simple cottage in a wood, perhaps a log fire . . . simple food and, of course, no technology; just well-chosen books and good conversation with beloved friends.

But that plainly polished wooden table needs to be sourced from an antique shop and polished hard every week to achieve the right patina. The flowers need changing every few days. That means someone has to go out and buy them or grow them in a garden. The bowl of fruit needs to be bought, cleaned and dusted. The cottage in the wood will be right at the top of the property market because everyone else wants one; and plumbing it into the mains will cost a fortune. You need a large car to get fuel for that simple woodstove to your door. You need a good education to tell the difference between bad books and good books for that elegant bookcase . . . when you begin to dig deep into the idealized image of the simple life, you realize that it is in fact very complex indeed. The dream of simplicity is more a matter of taste than of morality. It is also a kind of affluent showing off: the more minimalist the home, the more the owners seem to be telling the rest of us, 'We don't need to have a place to keep old board games, jigsaw puzzles, sewing materials, gift-wrap, Sellotape, spare duvets or next summer's shoes because we are so rich that when we need those things we just go out and buy them.'

The dream of the simple life began, indeed, in the eighteenth century with the super-rich: at one extreme, Marie Antoinette, wife of Louis XVI tried to arrange herself simply in a pastoral setting with the help of nineteen dozen flunkeys and a purpose-built toy hamlet; at the more practical, more politically correct end of the scale, the Lakeland poets opened the eyes of the comfortable English middle classes to the heart-stopping beauty of the countryside around them, so that the nation could fall hopelessly in love with it for a brief few decades before ruining it by building the M6. At both ends of the scale, for both queen and poet, it was necessary to enjoy financial security, education and a relatively good level of personal comfort in order to appreciate 'the simple life'.

Let us look around for someone who really does live a simple life. Our friend Jason is homeless and has been so for about 15 years. For as long as I have known him, which is about 10 years, he has lived in and out of various types of accommodation. Sometimes he gets thrown out of perfectly good places for being drunk and abusive, but most of the time he is pleasant and well mannered. He always has a smile for my youngest daughter, whom he has watched grow from a babe in arms to a big, sensible nine-year-old.

I ought to add that he has watched her grow from the vantage point of his regular position opposite the Underground station from which my daughter walks to school. For Jason is a professional beggar. I don't think he intended to end up as one, but it is the steadiest work he's ever done and he's pretty good at it.

His daily routine goes something like this: Morning: get up, get on bus to West End, take up regular begging pitch. Afternoon: move to afternoon begging pitch. Evening: purchase burger from fast food shop, something for the dog and a large bottle of cider. Nightfall: Go home to bed.

It's a very simple life indeed.

But it is not a particularly comfortable one. It is definitely not the sunset-streaked, wood-floor, open-plan dream of simplicity which you normally think of when those words pop into your head. And it is also a very unhealthy life: people who live on the streets die young.

Western mums and dads lead a very complicated life indeed in order simply to be comfortable. At the beginning of the Live

Simply week I was of the firm opinion that if I left behind a single spare pair of socks or mobile phone charger, then disaster would ensue: I would have to suffer the inconvenience of a non-working mobile phone – horror! – or some unfortunate person would have to wear the same pair of socks two days running – yuck!

We choose to lead a complicated life in order to be healthy; in order to meet the standards set by the society we aspire to. I could easily feed my children Jason's way, by stopping on the way home at a burger bar. Instead I try to buy organic food, plan weekly menus to ensure a full range of fresh foodstuffs is included in their diet, and make a gesture in the direction of the simple life by baking homemade bread (must be the RIGHT kind of special extra brown strong organic stoneground flour, of course).

Technology, too, is a great complicator of life. Advertisements for faster broadband connection never reveal the horrible and soul-destroying complexity of the helpline conversation which inevitably accompanies the installation. The slender girl in the magazine ad for broadband sitting at a minimalist table enjoying her cup of coffee and her laptop is strangely never depicted sitting, as I do daily, surrounded by yards of dusty cabling, piles of paper which represent the five hundred different things I have to get done this week, and dozens of discarded CD cases that can't be thrown away because they are not recyclable.

Nothing complicates life so much as the ever-spiralling pressure from the world of marketing and advertising. It is a cliché that we are under pressure to buy more, and to buy more often. Something very odd has happened to shopping itself. It used to be a household chore. Running errands for mummy used to be something you did to be helpful: that mummy needed errands to be run presupposes that mummy herself had found something more important to do at home.

Shopping is now no longer a task but a hobby, and a hobby which even children are persuaded to take part in – they see their 'celebrity' heroes pictured in magazines 'out shopping', with their harvest of designer carrier bags revealing where they have been, and assume that this is a pastime to be savoured: the spending of money on non-essentials becomes a spectator sport in its own right.

A bin liner

The life to which we are continually invited is being upgraded every year. Where our grandparents were smugly pleased to have an indoor loo, we feel embarrassed if we don't have a designer wet room shower. It is not enough for our children to eat fruit and vegetables every day: they must also eat only organic fruit and shiitake mushrooms, too.

Some people believe that these 'high production standards' are making us mentally ill, and there is even a word for it: affluenza.[1] Mental illness is on the increase in the UK, and professionals in the field reckon that the constant bombardment with media visions of perfect, unattainable homes, clothes, body images, careers, holidays, lifestyles is contributing to this increase. Many people who, if they lived in simpler societies with fewer aspirations, would be perfectly contented become discontented and unhappy because their own lives and their own abilities seem so dreadfully inadequate. We are all made to feel failures.

So the more complex life becomes, the more important it is that we, the parents of tomorrow's consumers, fight back with simplicity. We need to 'de-clutter from the inside out', stripping back our lives to the essentials. And the more we fight back, the better for our children — even for their future mental health.

The process starts with some inner de-cluttering — in the form of prayer. This prayer can take the form of just walking round the house looking at my possessions, asking myself, which of these objects do I really need? Which am I hanging on to out of habit? When did I last use that weird kitchen gadget that was meant to make professional-looking cookies, and in fact required the strength of ten to operate? What do my children need? What do I need?

And not forgetting the crunch question: If there were a fire in this room, and I had ten minutes, what would be worth saving?

Every now and again I arm myself with one black bin-liner, one green bin-liner and one of my local council's special recycling sacks and target a room in my house. If it is someone's bedroom I enlist their approval and help, but this is not always easy and anyway what I am going to describe is probably best done out of the sight of the room's owner. (I don't go near my husband's books, mind you. I am not *that* stupid.)

Into the *black* bin-liner goes pure rubbish. Into the *green* bin-liner goes anything which can be given away to a charity shop. Into the orange recycling bag goes anything which fits the local authority's narrow definition of a recyclable item.

Left to their own devices, children's bedrooms become slag-heaps composed of layers of discarded clothes, trainers, magazines, CDs, towels and computer games. Most of the clothes don't fit any more and the trainers have been pushed aside and are not worn because they look a bit dirty. The magazines have been sitting in the same pile, in the same order, for months, the CDs were listened to once and never again, the computer games are outdated.

Children do not instinctively see that discarded items can be renewed or reused. The clothes could be used by someone else, the trainers can be put in the washing machine, the magazines can be put in the recycling bag, the CDs given to a charity shop or swapped. But it takes a parent to point this out. Children normally solve the issue by kicking the object in question under the bed.

Undoubtedly the worst indictment of me, my mothering, my entire persona as a parent, is that pile of unwanted computer games. It is also an indictment of the society I live in. What was once the latest thing, to be desired and drooled over, is now merely the unwanted, unloved Version 1 in a system which has evolved all the way to Version 10. Every new technological tool for 'gaming' – notice the subtle change in use of a word that once meant specifically gambling – which is marketed to our children is designed *not* to last. When the new version comes out, the old version's games won't play on it. So out go the old games, and out goes the old gaming equipment. And in comes another lot, ratcheting up my children's expectations of what is 'required' to be contented, happy and pleasantly occupied.

These, too, go into the bin. Brave parents put the whole caboodle, console, screen and all, into the bin, and ban electronic games. Such parents are often also brave enough to venture through the twenty-first century without a television set.

That is unbelievably brave. I'm not ready for it. But any wimp of a mum can walk round the house with three bin-liners and make a start on de-cluttering, and anyone can ask him or herself the de-clutter-from-the-inside questions. You may not quite attain the simple life, but you will step an inch nearer.

Note

1. E.g., *Affluenza*, by Oliver James (London: Vermilion, 2007).

A candle (or fifty)   17

You are all children of light ...

1 Thessalonians 5.5

I have read many books telling me how to bring my children up better, and most of them have left me feeling a disorganized grouch, but none of them made me feel as inadequate as the electricity failure that hit our house at about seven o'clock one weekday evening.

For about an hour and a half, we had no power. Since we have a very elderly wiring system and two fuse boxes, one of them being in a very badly built annexe, this was ominous.

Our 17-year-old son emerged, growling, from the TV room. We had not seen him for quite some days, except briefly at meals. It took a power cut to flush him out. I expected him to begin howling with frustration at the sudden withdrawal of Sky TV, but instead he was eager to take charge. 'Give me the torch, Mum,' he said in a 'leave this to the man of the house' manner. 'I'll go and check the fuse boxes. 'I was impressed that he knew what fuse boxes were, let alone where to find them.

Our 15-year-old daughter was very anxious. She needed as much electricity as possible in order to carry out all her carefully laid, precisely calibrated plans for the evening. She likes to do her homework to high standards of presentation, and has a system of deadlines and backup deadlines for her various assignments, arranged on a neat wall chart: so she simply MUST be equipped with a computer with up-to-date software, and a printer for which an adequate supply of ink and paper is readily and constantly available. Only perfect office conditions are acceptable.

But without electricity, most of her homework simply could not be done. It was a horrible feeling for so well organized a person. She flipped through her neat and detailed diary and located a task that could be done with mere pen and paper. So, after lighting half a dozen candles and arranging them in a sparkling crescent around her exercise book, she set to work.

The two younger children behaved like cats in a thunderstorm. They prowled from room to room, unsure of what to do with themselves. The TV didn't work, the computers didn't work. After about an hour our nine-year-old settled happily having a parent read aloud to her, cuddling on the couch by the light of another crescent of candles. Our twelve-year-old, however, was almost in tears at being torn away from his computer game. Half an hour later he had forgotten his misery and was listening to the story with his sister.

Nothing could have brought home to me how dependent my children are on screens of various kinds – or rather, how dependent I have allowed them to become. When the older two were very tiny, we were an almost no-TV family. Then gradually we discovered lunchtime *Sesame Street*, and cartoons in the after-noon. Over the years, cartoons in the morning gradually crept into the daily routine, unchallenged, or insufficiently vigorously challenged.

One day it became no longer possible to watch important cricket matches on terrestrial channels, so Sky arrived – the excuse being that we wanted to watch JUST the cricket and the rolling news services. Sky stayed, even though we hardly ever have time to tune into the rolling news services, and the cricket is only a tiny percentage of the sports output.

At the same time, as the years went by and the children grew older, the number of computers in the house proliferated – both my husband and I work from home and our computers are our lifeline, but unfortunately it seems impossible to prevent them from accommodating computer games and so, somehow, the computer games sneak in. My husband and I never buy any computer games – they just appear in the house, like vermin. So now I have somehow ended up with children who are completely at sea without the TV or a computer.

Well . . . they are not *completely* at sea. The young are adaptable. One of the chief criteria for choosing a holiday house, from my point of view, is that it should have no TV, or at least only a very basic TV. As I have noted in Chapter 4, after 12 hours of moaning and moping the children go and find other things to do. And sure enough, the night the lights went out, the children were just about beginning to settle into finding other things to do when the lights went back on again.

A few weeks afterwards, the same thing happened: the lights all went out once more, only this time the power failure was uneven. The lights in the living room and kitchen worked, but none of the wall sockets or appliances, so we had no computers, no TV, no digital radio, no music, no cooker and no cooking gadgets.

With just the lights in the living room, however, we found that our power-cut experience was transformed. Once the boys had got over the fact that they were not going to be able to watch some essential football match or other, we simply made do.

Those who had homework were able to get on with it in good light, though again without computers. There was light for practising the piano and violin; I could not do ironing (hooray!), I could not put washing in the washing machine (double hooray!), or bake bread, but we could at least use the gas hob. And (unlike the previous episode) we could thoroughly appreciate electricity's loveliest gift: it means we can read books all evening without straining our eyes. So we ended the evening sitting around the kitchen table with hot chocolate while my eldest son read a Harry Potter book to us, beautifully, doing all the different voices just as well as Stephen Fry. We made the bathroom pretty with night-lights and each took a candle (under adult supervision) to bed. You don't need to see your face very clearly, I found, to wash it (though losing a contact lens by torchlight is disastrous).

The house had a stillness that reminded me of something – I wasn't sure what. Gradually I realized it was of my childhood in the 1960s. Even though we had TV and radio, there was no background hum. The machines in my house are an orchestra of hums. In the morning, before the electrician arrived, we noticed how the rooms of a house lit only from without – by daylight – feel dim and 'period'.

The kitchen table automatically became more important than ever because it was the most brightly lit place in the house. If their bedrooms suddenly cease to be electronic Aladdin's Caves, children with nothing to do gravitate towards the hearth (in other words, the kitchen) rather than being pulled away from it. It was as though our home had suddenly acquired a *centre*.

That evening showed us how we only need a very little electricity to be comfortable and happy. If we had made a conscious decision to switch off the lights, perhaps in some kind of 'live simply' exercise, then within twenty minutes we would have been switching on the TV to see the news, switching on a computer 'just to check our emails' – just because these things are there. Sure enough, next day we had full power and all the 'necessities' had to be switched on – the heating, the washing machine, the digital radio, the computers. We 'needed' all these things. But how restful it was for a few hours to be free of their magnetic force.

You cannot put the whole of your electricity supply into a black bin-liner and send it to charity, alas. But what about a 'power cut night' once or twice a month? It would mean going to your fuse box and flicking some of the switches to off, early in the evening. The aim would be to disable everything but the lights in your main living area (and the fridge) so that you can send yourself back through time.

This has been tried in Australia as a public statement about over-consumption of electricity, and it was a highly successful eco-stunt. The 'Earth Hour' was organized by the World Wildlife Federation of Australia in Sydney during the evening of 31 March 2007. Public landmark buildings such as the Sydney Opera House switched off their floodlights for the first time in living memory – in particular the non-essential lights which pick out the Opera House's famous silhouette against the night sky – and Sydney inhabitants switched off all the electricity they could do without for an hour. Streetlights and safety lights stayed on, but restaurants joined in the fun, offering 'candlelight dining', and an illuminated Coca-Cola advertisement in the middle of the city was switched off for the first time since it was switched on in 1974.

The inhabitants of Sydney were delighted with the novelty of the experience, especially the young. Many argued that some of the more public light displays ought routinely to be switched off for a few hours every night, say between 2am and 6am, to save energy.

When you turn out the lights, the first thing you notice is the sky. Children who live in the city are barely aware that the stars are there at night. Western cities are ridiculously over-lit and much of the light is wasted, directed upwards towards the sky: this wasted light serves no purpose but to blot out the stars.

Without darkness, we have no understanding of what light is.

In the Catholic Church, there is a tradition of the Easter Vigil. It is a Mass held in the middle of the night and always begins with the church in darkness. Everybody stands in darkness and then at the same time, at the moment that the Risen Christ is declared, candles are lit. The contrast is intense. Light becomes a profoundly precious thing, something to be adored and carefully husbanded instead of wasted. Some families enhance the experience by imposing a voluntary ban on switching on any lights during Easter Saturday, in order to know the complete darkness of a world without light: probably a more effective tradition if you live in the countryside far from the yellow glare of those streetlights.

Candles are used by some Christians to illustrate the passage of time through Advent and Holy Week. They are used in many Christian traditions to indicate a prayer said, a plea offered up. They are reminders of the epithet of Christ 'The Light of the World' and when placed on or around an altar they seem almost to guard it with their ring of light.

Candles are among the items in this Christian parent's toolkit that are not in the least bit symbolic. And they are cheap! Candles are the low-cost, environmentally friendly way of creating instant atmosphere.

Use them to create a sense of holy space, to focus a child's attention on what you are about to say: 'I'll light a candle and then we will talk all about it', is an enthralling way of opening a solemn or God-centred conversation. Candles create an atmosphere of stillness and cosiness like no other and act as an immediate signal that something special is about to happen. In Germany, candles are still routinely used in all homes to decorate Christmas trees, with a far more beautiful effect than our tawdry electric fairy lights.

As long as you are sensible, keep the matches out of reach and never let young children alone with them, using candles in the home can help teach youngsters how to handle things carefully and with respect. The more candles you have in the house, the more careful everyone needs to be! Here are some safety rules to remember:

- Only place candles on a stable, flat, heat-resistant surface and remember even nightlights can melt plastic.
- Keep them away from anything that can catch fire – curtains, little girl's plaits, lampshades, furniture … and away from draughts.
- Don't put candles under shelves – there can be a surprising amount of heat above a candle – it needs a metre clearance.
- Watch out for pets as well as children.
- Put them out when you leave the room.
- Never leave a candle or oil burner in a bedroom as the occupant goes to sleep.
- Use a snuffer to put them out, rather than blowing them out.

So now you have your lights turned out and your circle of candles, what are you going to do? Relax! Say some prayers. Read a passage of the Bible. Have a quiet moment while you think about the passage.

Then have some fun! Play a game or take turns telling stories. Keep those fuses switched to 'OFF' so that the kids can't wander off and switch on the TV. Finally, let them take turns snuffing out the candles and sit for a few minutes in the dark, thinking about the beginning of the world before God made light.

Look around the room and see how everyday objects are transformed when they are in shadow. Children who are afraid of the dark can see for themselves that nothing is inherently evil; it is simply the absence of light which makes them seem so. Shine the light into a dark, scary corner and it is revealed as no more than the place where the wastepaper bin is kept.

Gaze into the flame of the candle. How many colours can you see? How far does the candle's light reach? What shape is the flame like, and what makes it change and flicker? Make shadow puppets on the wall!

Have a candlelit dinner – not just for the parents or adults in the family but the children too.

A Story of the Venerable Bede

The English historian of the Dark Ages, the Venerable Bede, created the striking image of a bird flying in through one window into a firelit hall and then out through the opposite window to describe the mystery of our life here on earth:

> Such, O King, seems to me the present life of men on earth, in comparison with that time which to us is uncertain, as if when on a winter's night you sit feasting with your *earldormen* and *brumali* – and a simple sparrow should fly into the hall, and coming in at one door, instantly fly out through another. In that time in which it is indoors it is indeed not touched by the fury of the winter; but yet, this smallest space of calmness being passed almost in a flash, from winter going into winter again, it is lost to our eyes. Somewhat like this appears the life of man – but of what follows or what went before, we are utterly ignorant.

And so the darkness gathers round our little candle light on the kitchen table, and we think for a moment about how brief our lives are, and how mysterious is what lies around.

A storybook

18

Though the Witch knew the deeper magic, there is a magic
deeper still which she did not know ...
    C. S. *Lewis,* The Lion, the Witch and the Wardrobe

For more than ten years my children's lives were punctuated
annually by summer Potter Fever. More or less like clockwork, we
could rely on the end of the summer term being celebrated either
by the release of a new volume in J. K. Rowling's Harry Potter
series, or failing that, a film of one of the books she had already
managed to have biked round, fresh from her computer hard drive,
to the film script writers' offices for instant translation on to the
screen.

My children, in other words, grew up with the stories of Harry
Potter. Even children who would not normally pick up a book can
be persuaded to read one of J. K. Rowling's monstrous tomes. The
writing is not of the highest standard but the stories are gripping,
and the underlying messages – that love is more powerful than evil,
that sacrifice freely made is more powerful than force, that life is
sacred, yet death is not to be feared by the pure-hearted – are
perfectly in tune with Christian faith.

Children's fiction is more important than adult fiction because
the people who read it take it more seriously. Children who read,
even children who do not much like reading, remember their early
reading for ever. People who write for children soon become
aware of the impact their work makes: the impact of being the first
scratch on the clean slate. Unlike authors for adults, children's
authors are expected to subject themselves to the candid face-to-
face criticism of hundreds of their readers at public readings or
school visits. Unlike adult readers, children do not pretend to
admire an author they do not know, for the sake of looking clever,

nor do they flatter authors they do know. Children are a tough audience and it takes love and dedication to want to please them.

Some bad children's books survive, but only when kept alive by cynical publishers. The cemeteries of children's book publishing are littered with the corpses of books written badly by celebrities, books that were only purchased by people who were curious to possess a story with the celebrity's name on. These books normally sell well at first but have no staying power.

The story is often told of how many publishers rejected the manuscript of J. K. Rowling's first book, but – because the series subsequently received so generous a marketing budget and became linked with a succession of blockbuster movies – it is often forgotten that the first Harry Potter book (*Harry Potter and the Philosopher's* – in the USA, *Sorcerer's* – *Stone*) became well known purely by word of mouth in the playground. When it was published, my eldest son was eight and a highly competent reader for his age. One day, after finishing it he exclaimed, 'I wish I knew someone else who had read this book, then I could talk to them about it.' Within three months his wish was granted, not because of massive advertising but simply because the word had got round and all his friends were indeed reading the book – and this was before Christmas. Children spotted Harry Potter as a winner; adults were slower to pick up the message, particularly adults in the media.

After the publication of the second book, J. K. Rowling – who was still by then an approachable author and had not been hidden behind a high parapet of fame and security – allowed me to interview her in my home. Yes, she was so non-famous in that summer (1998) that she came to my house – not the other way around – simply because she needed a safe place for her small daughter to play while we talked.

Later, I contacted a national newspaper – were they interested in a J. K. Rowling interview? Oh no, the answer came. We've done her. We've moved on. It still had not really dawned on the adult world that something very big was about to hit the world of publishing in the form of J. K. Rowling. Yet all the children I knew at the time who had read the books could think of little else but when they might be able to read the next one. Not only had they virtually learned them off by heart, but were clearly going to be quoting from them and re-reading them into adulthood. Because they were good stories.

Not all children have been allowed to enjoy the Harry Potter phenomenon: many Christian parents believe that the books glorify magic and witchcraft. 'If they will not go for Harry Potter, what of the whole realm of fantasy and fairy tale?' says Sophie Masson, a children's author (*The Thomas Trew Mysteries*) based in Australia.

What indeed? If you refuse your child to read the most popular children's series ever written in case it encourages an interest in witchcraft, are you also prepared to ban the stories of Grimm, Perrault, Hans Andersen, all the way to Meg and Mog?

When C. S. Lewis's Narnia series first came out in the 1950s, some Christian parents banned their children from reading the books on the grounds that they were 'pagan' – i.e., there were too many Greek fauns, centaurs, dryads and so on. What such parents would have said if their children had announced an intention to read classical literature at university, or to study Greek sculpture, I don't like to think; in any case they looked extremely foolish when it became obvious to all that Narnia is an intensely Christian series written by one of the most successful Christian authors of his day.

Christianity thrives in art, and the art of narrative or story is its very lifeblood. Says Sophie Masson:

> because I'm a writer, I have always loved the fact that Jesus illustrated so much of his teaching and meaning through stories, and I have accustomed my children to look at meaning through story, not only Biblical stories but a very wide range. I think too many Christian parents seem frightened by stories, seem to think they somehow take children away from God whereas in fact the opposite may be much more true.

The Gospels indeed are nothing without narrative and story. No child can plough his way through the letters of St Paul; but put the stories of Jesus into a picture book and he's away. And not only the stories Jesus told have narrative power; so, too, does his own story. Here is a scene from one of those Narnia stories once condemned for their 'paganism': Lucy, the most beloved of the human children who visit the parallel and magical world of Narnia, finds herself looking through a book of spells in a wizard's house:

> On the next page she came to a spell 'for the refreshment of the spirit'. The pictures were fewer here but very beautiful. And what Lucy found herself reading was more like a story than a spell. It went on for three pages and before she had read to the bottom of the page she had forgotten that she was reading at all. She was living in the story as if it were real, and all the pictures were real too. When she had got to the third page and come to the end, she said, 'That is the loveliest story I've ever read or ever shall read in my whole life. Oh, I wish I could have gone on reading it for ten years. At least I'll read it over again.'
>
> But here part of the magic of the Book came into play. You couldn't turn back. The right-hand pages, the ones ahead, could be turned; the left-hand pages could not.
>
> 'Oh, what a shame!' said Lucy. 'I did so want to read it again. Well, at least, I must remember it. Let's see ... it was about ... about ... oh dear, it's all fading away again. And even this last page is going blank. This is a very queer book. How can I have forgotten? It was about a cup and a sword and a tree and a green hill, I know that much. But I can't remember and what *shall* I do?'
>
> And she never could remember; and ever since that day what Lucy means by a good story is a story which reminds her of the forgotten story in the Magician's Book.
>
> (C. S. Lewis *The Voyage of the Dawn Treader*)

The story which has entranced Lucy is, we are to understand, the story of Jesus' final days: the Last Supper, the meeting in the Garden of Gethsemane, the Crucifixion, the Resurrection. Lewis imagined that most children reading his books would have a basic Christian education and would pick up the references, or at least their parents would.

The cup which Lucy remembers is the cup from which Jesus and his disciples drank at the Last Supper, and of which Jesus said, 'Who drinks of this cup drinks of my blood.' The sword is presumably the sword which Peter drew in anger in the Garden of

Gethsemane, the tree is the cross on which Jesus was crucified and the green hill is the hill where it happened, and the sense of mingled loss and joy which Lucy feels is akin to the feelings which Jesus' disciples – and we – feel in knowing that he died, and then rose again. It is the perfect narrative (so perfect, that its most hostile detractors are convinced it's all made up) and Lewis' tribute to it is set right in the context of magic and wizardry: it is lurking in a book of spells, no less, for Lucy to find.

Whereas it is now fashionable to sneer at the 'preachiness' of C. S. Lewis's children's stories, it is usually adults who object, not children. Children mind less about being preached at, as long as the story is good and the preaching does not get in the way of its progress.

Stories are the way in which we express questions, and children do not necessarily mind if all the questions do not get answered within the story.

'Stories offer us a place to explore (as writers and readers) what it is to be fully human', says the author David Almond.[1] 'I do think that young people are interested in the major questions – Who are we? Where do we come from? Where are we going? Is there a God? – and they're willing to contemplate all kinds of possibilities. They haven't yet become tired by such questions.'

A literary sub-genre has grown up in Christian America (the 'Bible Belt'), devoted to opposing the Harry Potter books on the grounds that they promote witchcraft and magic and are anti-Christian. Other criticisms are piled in: that the children in the stories, for example, 'disobey authority' by sneaking out of their dormitories on missions. Presumably the same parents would greet with a nod of approval the Nazi concentration camp guards' claim, at the trials in Nuremberg, that they were 'only obeying orders'.

The overall theme of the Harry Potter books is the supremacy of love, and – finally – the power of self-sacrifice. In the final story of the series, Harry has to give himself freely in order to defeat the Satan-like Lord Voldemort. As in Lewis's *The Lion, the Witch and the Wardrobe*, a 'deeper magic' than that wielded by Lord Voldemort works to defeat him: the magic of love and sacrifice. Any Christian parent who cannot make something of these themes needs to buck up their imagination.

If we genuinely believe in God, we ought to believe that good stories, stories which have integrity, have something to say about the world God has created. God loves a good story, because He has told the best stories of all, and because good stories always hold a mirror up to his world.

It does not work to divide children's books into the Godly and the Ungodly on the basis of the subject matter (as Sophie Masson points out, ban magic from your child's bookshelf and you will have a very empty shelf) or because of the context.

If, on the other hand, you divide them into good stories on one side, and on the other side stories which are repetitive, formulaic, padded with inconsequential dialogue (alas, too many pages of the later Harry Potter books fall into that trap), obviously derivative or simply not telling an interesting story, then you are some way towards separating stories God loves from stories God hates.

A good story is one that reflects the truth: and Christians should never be afraid of the truth.

Note

1.   Interview by Random House Books.

Coffee and biscuits 19

What father among you, if his son asked for a fish, would hand him a snake?

Luke 11.11

I dreaded my delightful primary-school-age children growing up into teenagers. For one thing, children under 12 have proper bedtimes. And when they are young, children's bedtime is lovely – the snuggliest part of the day, with ritual storytelling, hugs and kisses, prayers and reconciliations. I also used to love the feeling of having 'left work' for the rest of the evening once the children were safely tucked in bed. My husband and I could settle down and almost pretend we were a young couple again.

How we yearn now for those days, the days when all our children went to bed earlier than we did. And it's no good telling them to go to bed at 10pm – they just don't seem to be able to. The other side of the teenage phenomenon of being completely unwakeable at 9am (see Chapter 22, 'An alarm clock') is a state of almost febrile alertness at 2am. And this is very often exactly when they want to stay up late and talk about their problems. 'You have to be prepared *to put in the late hours* with teenagers,' I was warned once by a mother of ten.

But, I protested; I adore my early nights. After a hard day's work I want to sit up in bed with a book and a cup of cocoa and my beloved husband. I don't *want* to have to schlep out to some party out in the suburbs to disentangle my daughter from some Boschian vision of hell masquerading as a birthday party; nor do I *want* to have to launch into a massive discussion of the rights and wrongs of euthanasia in the middle of the night. Darn it, can't they just go to bed at a proper time like me?

When these thoughts occur, I am allowing the 'false idol' (see Chapter 12, 'A kaleidoscope) of my personal comfort to block my view of my child, and of my relationship with my child. I realize that, in the long run, I will be glad I did the schlepping and the sitting-up, and the drinking of strong coffee to keep myself awake for the late-night taxi shift.

Once our children are old enough and confident enough to invite strangers into our homes, we feel the last vestiges of control melting away. The spectre of the all-weekend teenage party looms. A study by the Institute of Public Policy Research (IPPR) had found that British teenagers are the most badly behaved in Europe. The same study discovered, not to anybody's surprise, that there was a distinct link between how law-abiding, sociable and pleasant teenagers are, and how much 'quality time' they spend with their parents at home in the evenings, eating meals and 'just talking'.

Apparently unable to countenance the discomfort or incon-venience of spending time with our teenagers, we instead frighten ourselves to bits by reading scare stories about youngsters who invited their friends round when their parents were away, and ended up causing thousands and thousands of pounds' worth of damage. The IPPR has also concluded that more than in any other country, British adults are really scared of teenagers, more likely to move away because of their presence in the area, less likely to walk up to them and tick them off for misbehaviour.

Parents were on tenterhooks one summer when a Scottish rock musician, Calvin Harris, offered a prize of a free in-house per-formance for any teenager who had hosted the best party on a particular date in mid-August. Fears of an outbreak of all-night raves in which homes were wrecked ran like wildfire and parents were warned, 'stay at home on 18 August'.

There is more than a small element of bullying in this story – and how often is bullying disguised as teenage rebellion? The rock musician had the full support of his record company – no fly-by-night two men and a dog indie outfit, but Columbia, which is a subsidiary of Sony BMG. Sony BMG is half owned by Bertels-mann (the German-based company that owns several household American media names), and half owned by Sony Corporation of America. These are very big people indeed, putting around rumours that will enhance their music sales – rumours that frighten very small people for whom some broken windows and wrecked carpets represent real financial distress.

But do these parents perhaps partly deserve their distress? Do they bring it upon themselves from the day they allow communication with their teenagers to dwindle? It is noticeable that the main concern seems to be usually about damage to property by 'gatecrashers' (it's always gatecrashers ... never anyone the host teenagers will admit to knowing personally) rather than damage to human beings. Teenage boys are the group most vulnerable to physical violence, and unsupervised parties can turn ugly very easily; little is said, when parents talk of teenage parties, of the danger in which young people place themselves, much is said of the danger to ornaments and furniture.

In the light of horror stories about teenagers on the rampage, it seems paradoxical to suggest that parents need to make their homes more friendly to teenagers, not less. Yet Christianity loves a paradox and this is certainly the Christian response: when children try to discard our rules and make their own, we do not jettison our rules but we certainly need to look at what lies behind their requests and desires. 'What father among you, if his son asked for a fish, would hand him a snake? Or if he asked for an egg, hand him a scorpion? If you then, evil as you are, know how to give your children what is good, how much more will the heavenly Father give the Holy Spirit to those who ask him!'

The trouble is, if any teenage boy were to ask for anything half as healthy as an egg I would jump for joy. I would not only give him an egg, I would lead him to the fridge, show him where there's a box of a dozen eggs, butter, salt and pepper, and I would teach him how to make a scrumptious omelette for his friends as well. I would throw in a salad ... If only he would just *ask for the egg*. Or the fish. But he doesn't ask for eggs or fish ... he asks for snakes and scorpions. (Actually many teenagers would be deeply impressed to be given a pet snake or scorpion, and many teenage 'tribes' favour images such as scorpions on their jewellery, clothing and tattoos ...)

Without making the clumsy error of misreading a profound and sacred image of the power of prayer for simplistic parenting advice, that wonderful passage from Luke's Gospel does remind us that essentially we want the best for our children, and we *want them to want the best*. It also reminds us that we are not good parents if we hand them things that we know will hurt them. And perhaps we are not quite such good parents unless we show them what things will hurt them – unless we show them, to carry on Christ's arresting metaphor, the difference between a snake and a fish, a scorpion and an egg.

Unless we show them this difference we can't expect them to know there even is a difference; and if our homes are unwelcoming to teenagers in every way – if our homes are out of bounds not only to wild parties but also to any kind of teenage gathering because of our morbid fear that it might turn into a wild party – then they cannot be expected to learn how people of different generations can share a house together – and still, miraculously, relax and enjoy themselves.

But, you may protest, my home is incredibly teenager-friendly – too much so! We have Sky, we have broadband, we have Play-Stations galore. We have a constant stream of teenagers coming in and out. Half the time we don't know who is in the house and who isn't.

OK: the technology may be very attractive to teenagers, but is it there as much to placate as to welcome? And if you don't know who is coming in and out of your house, can you honestly say you are being friendly? By teenager-friendly I don't just mean comfortable. I mean a home that treats teenagers as friends rather than enemies or as strangers.

How do you treat your own friends – friends of your own age – and how do they treat you at your home? You don't say 'Oh, it's you,' when you see them on the doorstep; you don't offer them food which you know perfectly well they hate; when talking with them, you don't bring up subjects of conversation you know will make them feel awkward.

Whereas with teenagers it is strangely tempting to indicate grave disappointment at the very sight of their faces; to offer only food you consider healthy, just to spite the spoiled little brats . . . and it is tempting, too, to ask deliberately embarrassing questions, hoping to raise a laugh at their expense.

It is one thing to be friendly and welcoming to the *parents* of your teenagers' friends; but does your tone of voice change from cheery to sour when speaking to the kids themselves?

You may abhor the way they seem to constantly seek snack foods. But is this a big moral issue? As long as your teenager shares regular meals with the rest of the family, there is no harm in allowing for a generous snack food portion of the family budget. Then you can steer the visitors in the direction of the official snacking supplies without your own larder ending up looking as though locusts have been visiting. A monster biscuit barrel (probably with the words NOT FOR MUM inscribed on them in indelible ink), popcorn and a popcorn maker, soda drinks (yuck!), fruit, nuts – all very handy to have stashed away in industrial quantities where they can't be got at by vermin of the non-human variety. Not crisps though – too bulky!

Do you ever invite your teenagers to ask a friend in for supper? I know mine are very nervous about doing this – and to be honest I do not blame them, for on the occasions when our dinner table is not a scene of rage and misery, it turns into the Spanish Inquisition as the unfortunate guest is bombarded with questions. But I will keep *trying* to invite teenagers in, because I know it can be done – I do know families who break through the self-imposed generational apartheid that says parents and children may never, ever break bread together.

Do you have conversations in which you show, by listening, considering and not instantly contradicting, that you value their opinions? Do you ask them what they think about the latest film or the big story in the news? Do you remember your kids' friends' names, do you ever make a note of their likes and dislikes, what they are up to, where they go on holiday? You can learn quite a lot from them, and I don't mean just about teen 'culture'.

Is there part of the house – whether family room, garage or shed – where they can hang out without being under your feet? Well, lucky you. If you don't have that kind of space, what about agreeing with your teenager that they can have the living room on a fixed couple of evenings a week, no arguments, as long as you have prior claim over it for the rest of the week?

Is your personal comfort more important than keeping in touch with the teenager? Our personal comfort may become a very insidious obstacle. I know this because nearly every evening I think of tackling my teenager about his homework ... but decide against it, because I don't want him shouting at me again. When this happens, I am putting my comfort first, not him. Every night I can't be bothered to go and say goodnight to him before I go to bed, I am putting my comfort first, not his. Every time a father orders his teenagers to go out with their friends because he really wants the house to himself for a 'bit of peace and quiet', he is probably putting his own comfort first, not his children's.

A little flexibility allows you a clear conscience in setting out the rules you do care about. Contrary to the opinion of most teenagers and, alarmingly, most parents in the UK, it is perfectly reasonable to have house rules prohibiting alcohol, smoking, drugs and sex. It is perfectly reasonable to ask for respect on these points – as long as you offer some genuine respect back. And teenagers do grow into adults very quickly. It is simply a matter of managing to stay awake long enough for it to happen ... and that's where the strong coffee comes in ...

A pair of hiking boots 20

After saying goodbye to them he went off into the hills to pray.
Mark 6.46

In Jesus' world, life was conducted outdoors. Indoors was dark and ill-lit, smoky and not particularly comfortable. If you wanted to get a difficult bit of work done, you took it out into the bright Mediterranean sun and did it there. If you wanted to lounge around, you found a nice bit of grass or a rock.

In Mel Gibson's famous (and infamous) film, *The Passion of the Christ*, there is a curious scene in which Jesus knocks up a dining table and his mother Mary says it will never catch on. The Fred Flintstone-esque humour of this scene may be a little clumsy, but it does serve to underline how underdeveloped was the idea of 'indoors' for people of Jesus' world.

And right through until the Industrial Revolution, and certainly until gaslight and electric light, most of us even in the dark and rainy North spent our working lives outdoors. As the Monty Python writer turned historical novelist Terry Jones engagingly observed at the opening of one of his novels set in medieval times, it was very hard to run away from a medieval village because everybody was outside, working, and would only have to look up from their work to see you walking away from the village: they were not indoors watching the telly.

Now we live most of our lives indoors. We have to because so much of what we do is driven by electricity. Forced indoors by technology, we are cut off from the rest of the world so powerfully that it takes a lot to make us even look out of the window. Yet outdoors is God's world; indoors everything is ordered by man. Indoors, we are in the narrow and pre-planned little world which humans construct for themselves, imagining themselves to be kings of the universe. Outdoors we see that little world for what it is – a *little* world. Outdoors is organic, growing, unpredictable, often windy and wet, difficult, awkward, uncomfortable; indoors is neat, organized, tidy, dry and arranged for comfort.

'Walking with children is useful for being spacious in your mind and thinking more widely,' says Kate, a mother of three and an Anglican. She finds that it is on walks that her children begin having their most interesting discussions about God, faith, their future plans, their friends and worries.

Because I live in the middle of London my opportunities for walking are limited to parks – but the parks we have access to are nonetheless quite big enough to prove Kate's thesis that walking creates 'space in your mind and thinking more widely'. Being an inveterate and thoroughly nosy eavesdropper, I love strolling through Kew Gardens and overhearing the conversations other people are having. Very often I hear a snatch of a very deep, personal conversation. People bring visiting friends or relatives to the park, they walk along the graceful paths and flower-bedecked dells, and within twenty minutes they have got away from their small talk and begun talking about the things that are really bothering them. Near the gate, where people come in, we hear snippets of lightweight chitchat; down in the woodland glade or the rhododendron dell, the talk is of love, life, death, and how will Mother cope on her own.

For while going out for a walk undoubtedly puts us in touch with the natural world, it also seems to help us to open up our own inner world more easily. It is something to do with the choreography of a walk. Normal awkwardnesses in conversation – especially with teenagers – can be smoothed over when you are all walking along and there are different things to look at and point out; your teenager can walk a little apart if he wants to, yet still be part of the group; your small child can skip backwards and forwards and explore tree roots and rabbit holes.

The decline in walking to school is having catastrophic consequences for children's health and fitness; but what about their mental and spiritual development? Little is said of this. Yet some studies[1] have shown that the more we drive our children around, the more we stunt their ability to cope with situations on their own. We strip them of opportunities to learn to be sensible. We stunt their independence. Younger children need to be able to explore the less planned, less predictable world of outdoors. Older children need to be tempted away from the manmade delights of computer games. And if we stunt children's ability to think for themselves, surely we stunt their spiritual development, too?

Your local area may have schemes such as Safe Routes to School, Walking Buses or School Travel Plans which will help you to devise a walk-to-school plan for your child. The exercise is great, and children who walk to school are even said to improve academically. And, point out the Ramblers' Association, children who walk to school and back are better prepared for more interesting and adventurous walking during weekends and the holidays.

For it is undoubtedly during the school holidays that getting your kids out for a walk is the simplest way to banish the blues, end squabbles and improve tempers all round. It is very simple to do and requires minimum kit. They will almost always be reluctant to set off – especially in winter – but will return home with bright eyes and a sense of triumph.

And if you get soaked once in a while, so what? Children rarely have much exposure to the elements. It is surprising often to find how timid city children are. Small children are actually unintentionally taught in nursery to be afraid of rain – rain is the disaster at the end of every picture book, the cause of dismay in nursery rhymes. Yet without it we cannot survive. A bit of rain, children need to discover, does not actually hurt and is even refreshing when you've been getting hot and dusty on your walk.

So I am putting into the Christian parent's toolkit a pair of hiking boots. Wellingtons would be OK as a substitute, especially if you are going to pass through puddles and streams, though they need to be checked for fit as nothing is worse than wearing ill-fitting boots on a long walk, except possibly being the parent who has to carry the child with the ill-fitting boots. Also you will need a rucksack, a lightweight waterproof per person, and if you have a baby or a toddler, then that wonderful invention, the all-terrain buggy, will give you the freedom of the hills.

Of course, the first rule for walking with children is to avoid using the words 'going for a walk' which sounds pointless and tame. At the very least talk of 'going for a hike', even better suggest to your children that they come out for an 'adventure', go on a 'mission to discover a secret location' on the map, go exploring . . . any concept that will get imaginations racing. But 'go for a walk'? Boring!

Give some thought to the map reading. If necessary write the route instructions out and give them to the kids. Boys especially love and respond to maps – it is a cliché, but it has also been shown by educational psychologists to be true. Nominate a child – preferably the more disaffected and grumpy of the troupe – as map-reader for the day (though have a duplicate map tucked in your pocket, for discreet reference) and print off routes from internet walking websites for each child to carry.

Take snacks and drinks and ration them out as rewards for achieving another leg of the journey. Curious specialist sweets like Kendal Mint Cake will make you feel like real mountaineers, even when you are really in Berkshire. Always carry water, a bottle per person, especially in the summer.

Choose circular routes wherever possible. It is fun coming back to the place you started out, only from a different direction. Until their legs are as long as yours, let the age in years of the youngest child be the guideline for the maximum distance you can expect, in miles.

Let the children dictate the pace. Try not to hurry or harry them – being frogmarched is boring, and so is being told to 'come ON' every five minutes. One dad suggests setting the pace – not too fast – at the start of the walk, to establish a steady speed, and then letting the children set the pace towards the end.

Give them a digital camera and encourage them to take dozens and dozens of photographs. You can delete the ones of their feet and keep the good ones to put in a hiking scrapbook.

Choose walks with varied landscape, especially woodland or anywhere with rocks and slopes. Sadly my own favourite landscape – a stretch of windswept sandflats at low tide – is far too boring for most children so I generally wander along it alone.

Set challenges: who can collect the biggest number of different tree-leaves in the day? Who can spot the biggest number of different birds? My youngest child was covered in glory (as well as scratches) one summer when she stumbled through a thicket and spotted a real live adder slithering away.

A pair of hiking boots

One family of experienced hill-walkers reports: 'We look for Dragon Nests (cairns), Witch's Knickers (plastic bags) and Gollum's Poo (thank you sheep)!'

The games my family play on walks rarely rise from the basic hiding-behind-a-tree-and-jumping-out-going-boo level, but there are more sophisticated alternatives. If one adult sets off half an hour before the rest of the party, they can lay a treasure trail or leave secret signs like crossed branches or piles of leaves in the path, which the others have to collect. With small children who are flagging on dull stretches of featureless road, try a burst of 'follow my leader'.

When we take our children outdoors, even if only for a walk down the road or across the local common, we put ourselves under the sky. We become aware of how small and insignificant we could be and also aware of how at each step we have the power to destroy or preserve the landscape. Going outdoors, we have the space to look up and feel intimate with the sky; reflecting that each of us is loved by God individually.

Note

1. E.g., Mayer Hillman's seminal *One False Move* (London: Policy Studies Institute, 1990).

Stacking chairs

21

For where two or three meet in my name, I am there among them.

Matthew 18.20

A church is not just a church. Recently the architectural historian Sir Roy Strong called for Britain's village communities to rip out the pews (the heavy, fixed, wooden benches traditional in England since the eighteenth century) from their medieval parish churches so that the buildings could conveniently double as community halls where dancing, parties and other fun could take place.

Sir Roy's remarks came from the viewpoint of a man concerned mainly with preserving architecture rather than with preserving faith, though respectful of the latter. 'To me, in heritage terms, just as the twentieth century was about saving the country house, the twenty first century will be about saving our great historic churches,' he said.[1]

Sir Roy's observation of what is wrong with the 10,000 rural churches that dot our countryside is that whereas in the past, they were living, busy, noise-filled hubs of activity, living reflections of the ups and downs of the community to which they belonged, in the twenty-first century they are used only for a few hours a week by a small proportion of the local population. And this is quite clearly not enough.

He added: 'The majority of the population has no idea what goes on in a church or even more what used to go on in a church in other centuries. Those of you who have been present at a service of thanksgiving where the service sheet has failed to print the words of the Lord's Prayer will know exactly what I mean.'

The Church of England is still technically an 'established' church, but its leaders are painfully aware of how little this relates to reality. Dr Michael Nazir-Ali, the Bishop of Rochester, has spoken of the 'chilling spiritual vacuum' he perceives in Britain. He says: 'It struck me at the moment in [Princess] Diana's funeral [in 1997] when the archbishop led the congregation in The Lord's Prayer. The cameras went to the masses of people outside. They could start it. But they couldn't get beyond the second line.'[2]

Sir Roy's call to 'rip out the pews' hit the headlines for a day, but was not as outrageous as some of the reaction to it seemed to imply. It is not quite as practical as he probably thinks it is because chairs are ugly and uncomfortable, especially for children; but it isn't as radical as the news editors seemed to want to believe.

The medieval church did not even have pews; the nave, the main body of the church where you and I usually sit, was an open space. People in the medieval, Catholic, pre-Reformation days did not expect to be able to sit down wherever they went, and the church was the only well-built, weather- and attack-proof building in the village besides the local castle. So, by providing what architects would now call a free-flowing inner space, it was used for meetings, elections, auctions, legal proceedings and festivities.

The church even offered a good, dry storage space for the village fire-fighting equipment, the ducking stool and the stocks, not to mention doubling up as the village armoury. The sacred part of the church was kept separate, but not completely hidden, by means of the rood screen, that wonderful pierced wooden structure which graces so many churches and showcased the talents of the English carpenter at the height of his powers ... and that well-meaning twentieth-century parsons ripped out because they wanted to bring the congregation and the sacred space of the altar together. Too bad that just as the rood screen was being ripped out, the congregation was beating a steady and silent retreat via the door.

As Sir Roy has pointed out, there is no guide to English churches which presents the church as a place of community rather than a place of architecture and history. Instead, the most popular recent guide was a book by the distinguished journalist Simon Jenkins called *England's Thousand Best Churches*. Jenkins proclaimed at the beginning of the book that as far as he was concerned 'a church is not a place of revealed truth but rather a shrine of impenetrable mystery, symbol of humanity's everlasting quest for explanation'. He takes exception to notices in churches of great beauty which plead 'This building is not a museum, it is a place of worship', pointing out that churches are indeed museums 'and should be proud of the fact. No apostolic faith can renounce its past.' He calls for churches to be taken care of not simply by the Church of England but by the whole community, the faithless as well as the faithful.

There is something wrong with this kindly, scholarly way of regarding churches. How alienated do we have to be from our past to think it is civilized to walk into a place used daily for worship, and simply gaze critically at the architraves as though walking into a museum? How can the faithless be expected to support the 'fabric' of the church unless some of them are drawn into its living, loving worship?

I have always secretly longed for there to be more guides to churches which told us what really went on inside. Ideally it would be aimed at the secular market yet not exhibit the faith-blindness of so many secular guides. It would explain the architecture, but at the same time offer information about the type of congregation and worship at each church. It might even help to steer the aesthetically highbrow away from churches where the enthusiastic folk-singing would offend their ears, and it would also steer the socially conscientious away from churches where architecture is unashamedly adored.

Our church recently had all its pews sent away for repair and refurbishment. They were replaced temporarily by village-hall-type plastic chairs with aluminium legs that screeched and groaned across the floor tiles every time they were moved. We hated them. Every time one moved, the chair would shift and rattle, and after every Mass the sacristan's neat rows had turned into waves, like the ripples in tide-washed sand. Watching one adorable toddler creating complete anarchy by delightedly rearranging all the chairs within reach during one Mass, my teenage daughter nudged me and whispered, 'That's why we have pews ...'

But then, this small impractical aspect of Sir Roy's proposal – an aspect I am sure that could be overcome by clever chair design – only highlights the difference between the church I attend – a thriving inner city church of the Roman Catholic persuasion, where the requirement for weekly Sunday Mass attendance is still a definition of practice, and the kind of church Sir Roy knows in his lovely rural Herefordshire: fine medieval buildings in which a tiny handful of very old people meet every few weeks or so and where a child is hardly ever seen; churches which are still suffering the long-term effects of the depopulation of the countryside during the Industrial Revolution.

Cities are notoriously impersonal. The one thing every person misses in a city is the sense of belonging to a community. So everyone who comes to a city tries instinctively to find their own community.

Immigrants bond together with friends-of-friends-of-friends and form contacts and close bonds with people they would never have give the time of day to, back home. Young people seek the places where they will see, and be seen with, the kind of people they want to become.

And worshippers find places of worship. A place of worship provides, or should provide, an instant community for the new-comer and an established, trusted community for the long-time resident. There is no other meeting point in modern society today to touch a church, or almost any other place of worship, for this amazing quality. There is no other forum or social gathering where your child will meet the same across-the-board mixture of people.

For at school, your child meets only children of her own age, unless she is taught in a 'vertically grouped' setting in a small rural school. If she is one of the 10 per cent of British children who attend a private school, the children from whom she selects her friends will come not from all income brackets or all walks of life, but from the upper income bracket only.

The range of people whom your child encounters in social gatherings is also self-selecting, because they all fall roughly into the category of people that you call your friends and the friends of your friends. This set of people, however you look at your friendships, is exclusive rather than inclusive, and people can be dropped out of it just because they are not particularly popular.

In a church, on the other hand, your child will meet the young and the old, the rich and the poor, people of all races, people of all educational levels, people from all walks of life. Your child will learn to stand at the altar alongside the reformed drug addict and the social worker, the soldier and the pacifist, the hedge fund manager and the shop assistant.

'Nowadays everyone is fretting about social fragmentation. If you go to a Catholic parish on a Sunday, you'll see the opposite of that. You'll see people of all races and ages, and social class, coming together to share something really profound. And making a common identity for themselves. Every parish has the potential to be a neighbourhood Utopia',[3] says Frank Cottrell Boyce, the screenwriter. And to some extent, does this not apply to churches of all denominations?

Your parish church is, on the most mundane level, an instant village. If it is well run it should offer some kind of activity for people of all ages and with as wide a variation of needs as possible. There should be something for the old, something for couples, for singles, for young adults and for teenagers – and opportunities for all of these to cross paths. If the church is empty, it is not because of loss of faith; it is because people have stopped expecting to meet each other there.

Yet the church, for those who adopt it as their village, is a ready provider of routine and security: 'The children like [the fact] that I go to church. It makes them feel safe within the week, I think,' mused a mum of three teenagers.

Simon Jenkins disagrees with churches that do not want to be regarded as museums, because he thinks this means they want to ignore their past. Yet the liturgical life, the rhythm of worship, is mapped out with a church calendar, a calendar that was planned out centuries ago. That calendar is a direct link with the past in a way that the museum information cards which Mr Jenkins suggests should be put up inside churches could never be.

The church calendar also tracks the change of seasons for us; and its pre-decided series of readings takes us on a train of spiritual thinking that few of us would venture on ourselves. If I were left to my own devices every week to choose which spiritual text to read for myself, I would undoubtedly skip the difficult ones and go for the easy bits, every time. I might just end up reading *Heat* magazine or the Sunday papers instead. I do not think I am alone in this.

And the church, whether still, noisy, decrepit or magnificent, modern or ancient, always is a place where the mundane meets the eternal. That mixture of races, ages and classes to which Frank Cottrell Boyce alludes is there to do something profound; they are standing in the middle of their instant village hall, opening a door on to the infinite.

Notes

1. 'The Beauty of Holiness and its Perils: What is to Happen to 10,000 Churches?', Gresham Lecture by Sir Roy Strong, DLitt, PhD, FSS, on 30 May 2007.
2. Quoted by Brian Moynahan in 'Praying for a Miracle', *Sunday Times Magazine*, 27 May 2007.
3. Quoted in *Why I am Still a Catholic*, edited by Peter Stanford, London and New York, Continuum.

An alarm clock   22

Peter and his companions were heavy with sleep but they kept
awake and saw his glory.

For most of us it's more a case of 'good God, it's morning' than
'Good morning, God!' We need to stay awake. A daily act of
self-denial is a reminder of God and of who we really are. One
way is to dedicate every new day to God by spending a few
minutes in quiet prayer, especially as we wake.

Archbishop Vincent Nichols, Archbishop of Birmingham
*(*Walk With Me – Lenten Journey 2007*)*

Every morning, when you wake up, try saying, 'What have you
got for me to do today, Lord?'

Fr Jason Gordon, Trinidad, in conversation with my children

Marie Stubbs (Lady Stubbs) is a terrific teacher and a very Christian
woman who was given the unenviable task of pulling back together a failing inner city comprehensive school, St George's in
Maida Vale, where in 1995 a headmaster was murdered outside the
school gates. One of her main weapons was the alarm clock. She
had boxes and boxes of them in her office, and if pupils were
persistently late for school they would be invited to her office
where they would be presented with an alarm clock as a gift.

Children need the inevitability of certain things happening
throughout the day: getting up time, breakfast time, school time,
bath time, bed time. So for this toolkit, the alarm clock is essential.
It is a symbol of the rhythm of routine which children find so
comforting. No arguments about that.

In hypnotherapy, we use certain routine words or actions as

'anchors', reminders that help to set our thoughts off on the positive track where we want them to go. It is not possible for a word or action to become an anchor after just one or two repetitions – the human mind needs multiple repetitions before it gets the message. By setting down ideas of punctuality and routine in childhood, we help children to learn to set 'anchors' along their journey through the day.

According to some medical experts, adolescents find getting out of bed physically much more difficult than the rest of us. Their developing brains need more sleep, and at the same time they find it harder to go to sleep early in the evening than everyone else.

Apparently, in late puberty, a hormone called melatonin, which seems to be related to our ability to sleep, is secreted at different times of day from its pattern earlier and later in life. The melatonin issue seems to give rise to a basic design flaw in teenagers: while parents are ready for sleep by 10pm, the household teenager literally cannot fall asleep until 2am.

But at the same time, infuriatingly, your teenager needs a lot more sleep than anyone else under the age of about two. Teenagers can't help it – it's just the way they are. So the boy who once bounced out of bed and began running around playing superheroes at 6am is now quite unwakeable until midday. He is not being deliberately lazy; he is not necessarily depressed, even though he may appear so. He just needs to catch up on his sleep.

Scientists have not clarified exactly what the genetic or anthropological purpose of this aspect of adolescence is, which leaves the field open for us amateurs. Here is my theory: quite obviously, teenagers are nature's night-watchmen.

While older cavemen and cavewomen preferred to go to sleep at a sensible time, they could rest easy in their nests knowing that the cave-teens were up and about long into the small hours, terrifying the local predators away from the camp fire by their sullen, moody appearance. Cave parents did not fret about their children's sleeping habits, muttering 'what time do you call this, then?' I am sure that cave parents used their teenagers for the purpose nature intended. Naturally hostile, automatically threatening in aspect, and lacking (apparently) in communication skills or empathy with other creatures, teenagers are ideally suited for the job of staying up alone in the dark staring into the flames of the camp fire, striking fear into the hearts of strangers.

We should be making more use of our teenagers' nocturnal habits. By wanting them to conform either to the tidy bedtimes of their childhood or to the sensible regularity of their parents, we approach teenagers and sleep habits completely from the wrong angle. So why not install night rate electricity and teach them how to load the washing machine, hang out the washing and do all the ironing in the small hours of the morning? 'And don't you go to bed until every one of these shirts is ironed!'

Think of all the things your teenager could do while you sleep, all the useful household tasks that could be accomplished. Vacuuming the living room might be a bit noisy at 2am, but what about making healthy vegetable soups and smoothies for the freezer, something few parents ever have time to do? Baking cookies for the lunchbox? Just leave the ingredients out on the counter with a set of extremely detailed step-by-step instructions, go to bed and let them get on with it.

Goldfish, guinea pigs and cats don't mind what time of day they get fed, so your nocturnal adolescent can usefully be employed in routine pet care during the midnight hours.

Am I serious? Partly, yes. I do wish our society had a better idea of what to do with teenagers besides targeting them with the marketing of useless electronic games and gadgets. I wish we could be more honest about what we want from them: on the one hand we worship youth, and on the other hand we recoil from it when confronted with it red-eyed and bleary, with chip-grease stains down its front and newly sprouting acne on its nose. Our marketing and media industries worship youth so frantically that female newsreaders over 50 are banished from the screen; yet at the same time we are afraid of young people, especially strange young people who we fear may be carrying knives. There is certainly a need for young people to feel more important in the sense that they feel more responsible.

The alarm clock also serves as an image of the state of wakefulness and watchfulness in which Christians are told to be, in the manner of the wise virgins who looked after their lamps properly so that they didn't fall over themselves in the dark when the bridegroom arrived (Matthew 25.1–13). It is a beautiful and exciting concept, the idea that every minute could be the most important minute of your life. It makes life feel so rich and full; not boring and flat at all. It is a terrible paradox: the more comfortable the life, the less the person living it will value the sheer beauty of being alive. Having children is a wonderful part of being alive. Having children wake you up at 5am is a wonderful part of being alive, simply because it is part of having children. And having children bring you burnt toast and 'tea' made with cold water on Mother's Day is just the most wonderful part of being alive known to humankind.

The God bag 23

> People were bringing little children to him, for him to touch them. The disciples scolded them, but when Jesus saw this he was indignant and said to them, 'Let the little children come to me ...'
>
> *Mark 10.13–14*

The alarm clock has another very important role to play in the Christian parent's toolkit. It is needed every Sunday morning, and needs to be set to go off when everyone else is still on their biological snooze button. For not even Lady Stubbs had what I consider the ultimate time-keeping challenge: getting kids out of bed on Sunday mornings in order to go to church.

The problem is not so bad when children are small, believe it or not. Provided you are not so foolish as to allow your children a choice about coming with you to church when they are small, then for as long as you are bigger than them you ought to be able to chase your children out of the house somehow, even if once in a while you arrive at the church with at least one child wearing pyjamas. The problems arise when the kids get large, and heavy, and independent minded.

Sunday morning is the time of the week when Christian families feel most different from the secular world. Everyone else is snoozing until ten or eleven, and the Sunday morning lie-in seems to have become some kind of ancient right enshrined in the Magna Carta. Meanwhile my family and I are up, breakfasted and out with our children in time for church – a juggling act which never fails to amaze me. I notice that my children have always been very insistent about avoiding any activity that requires an early start on *Saturday* morning, because they regard this as their only proper weekly opportunity for a lie-in.

Is getting up to go to church worth it? Of course it is.

Christianity is not something you do by yourself. It is not a private affair. Christ said that wherever two or three of us were gathered in his name, he would be there with us. This is a faith that requires us to make contact with others. Without contact with others, faith becomes navel-gazing self-admiration.

You can, if you prefer, go down the 'personal spirituality' route. You can go to your local bookstore and pick up any one of a thousand books about 'spirituality' which give you permission to focus entirely on your inner self, your inner well-being, your inner child, your inner world, your inner rabbit for all I know. Focusing on your inner self is great fun. There is nobody to argue with and you can spend all the time with your favourite person. It is the spiritual equivalent of Woody Allen's definition of masturbation: 'sex with someone I love'. It is in this kind of spirituality, as Chesterton remarked, that 'Jones worships Jones' (see Chapter 2, 'A road map').

One of the ingenious things about Christianity is the way it forces us to swallow our pride and go out to meet other people. Forced to make contact with others, we are also forced to make compromises, listen to other points of view and above all look out for other people's needs: and only when we do these things are we putting Christ's most powerful commands into action. Silent contemplation is a vital part of our spiritual life, but on its own it is not enough. We need a bit of feedback from the rest of society and we cannot call ourselves followers of Christ unless we are open to worshipping alongside other people – even people we wouldn't have chosen as friends, normally – and to helping others.

Which is a long way of saying that it is really, really important to set the alarm clock on Saturday evening, to go off in good time on Sunday morning when everyone wants a lie-in.

Perhaps by now you've discovered a church you feel comfortable with and where you are fairly sure your children will be welcome. Now here comes the difficult bit: every Sunday morning you are destined to get up early, get your family up, breakfasted and dressed and off to church, and then somehow survive an hour-long service in the company of your fellow Christians and your cross or bored children.

This is the experience that for several years of my life left me feeling I'd done several rounds in the ring with Frank Bruno rather than offered up my prayers to my Lord. Isn't it enough, we mutter, to get children to school five days a week with lunch money/packed sandwiches/PE kit/geography project/charity donation/permission slip for school outing all intact, without having to go through another version of the same torment on a Sunday?

In the early days, now and again, I would roll over in bed at 8.45 on a Sunday morning (45 minutes to lift-off time) and say to my husband, with the distinctive croak of the genteelly hung-over partygoer in my voice, 'Oh can't we just miss church this once?'

And once or twice he gave in and we did miss church. The children played happily through Sunday morning just like everyone else's children. I got the Sunday lunch in the oven nice and early and did a bit of gardening. Lovely.

Next Sunday, boy, did we pay for it. Because when one part of any routine is missed out, the first lesson small children learn is that this part of the routine CAN be missed out. One relaxed Sunday is paid for, the following Sunday, by more yelling, nagging, dragging-back of duvets, pleading, bribing and ordering than we've needed in – well, in a month of Sundays.

Children are excellent philosophers and logicians and understand the difference between the *a posteriori* and *a priori*; having observed that church may be deleted from the regular Sunday, they conclude that church is therefore not a necessary part of Sunday: you may miss out going to church and the sun will still rise, the earth will still spin on its axis. In which case (any intelligent three-year-old will surmise) why bother to go THIS Sunday if we didn't bother LAST Sunday?

The TV schedules are not on our side. Sunday morning TV programmes for young children are intended to allow the non-churchgoing parents another hour or two's snoozing. The wrap-around format which is the pattern for early morning children's weekend TV scheduling is deliberately created to draw the child into an artificial party atmosphere which seems, to the child, a delightful and easy substitute for church. Early on in our parenting journey, we got the message: if we just ONCE relaxed the rule about church on Sunday, then we were in for trouble later on. So reluctantly (on my part at least) we would drag ourselves out of bed and dress two, then three, then four children who all far preferred to be watching Sunday morning TV, and somehow get them to church, usually more or less on time.

Here are some tips for getting that Sunday morning feeling over with:

- Keep Sunday special. No, I don't necessarily mean campaigning for shops to shut on Sundays. I just mean that if you make Sunday a pleasant day for the whole family, from the moment the alarm clock goes off, then it all seems worthwhile. Sunday is a feast day: so feast!
- Be positive. Church is NOT a punishment. It is worship, spiritual refreshment, the centre of our week. If you don't look forward to it, why should your children?
- Get Sunday clothes (not 'Sunday best', please!) ready the night before so that you can all just slide into them half asleep in the morning. Or go to church in pyjamas.
- Promise a specially reserved breakfast treat that is just for Sundays.
- Promise a special ritual after church that everyone likes the sound of – the favourite café, family pub, walk through the park.
- Try to get your household chores, home office chores, bill-paying, shopping, perhaps even gardening, out of the way, so that the only real duty (as opposed to pleasure) you have left over for Sunday is worship. This is an approximation of the strict Jewish pattern of Sabbath observance, and it is a wonderful time-management tool because it forces you to get work done in LESS than the time available – a kind of mirror-image of Parkinson's Law.[1]

Prepare ye the way of the breakfast

There are mothers and fathers out there who routinely lay breakfast tables before they go to bed. Not many of us have a full-scale breakfast table these days; all the same, it does pay to get out what you know you need regularly and have things where everyone can reach them. On a dodgy Sunday morning, every time a kitchen cabinet door does not need to be opened is another head saved from banging on it by accident – that's my motto.

Know your journey

Be aware not only of exactly how long it takes to get to your church but how long it takes to park and make it to the door. Avoid planning to do any errands on the way to church.

The God bag

Somewhere near your front door there should be a bag whose sole raison d'être is to go to church and come back home again. In this bag is a selection, frequently updated, of more or less religiously themed books, some crayons and colouring materials, a bottle of water, tissues. Also, if you are really organized, collection money and the parish magazine. Instead of scouring the house for something to amuse your child, you have a pre-planned selection of bits and pieces that have the slight but significant increase in novelty value imparted by the fact that the child hasn't seen them for a week.

Velcro marbles

I know you can't really buy Velcro marbles but wouldn't they be a great idea? Imagine the quiet and harmless games that two small children could have with such a toy . . . sticking them to the coats of adults in the pew in front, playing silent games of bowls on the floor . . . the possibilities are endless.

Better late than never

Leaving the house with small children, especially babies, is complicated. Even if you are running ten minutes late, don't give up just because you'll be late. Just get there, and make a bit of an effort next time. And if you are on time every week, and you grind your teeth when other families burst into church 20 minutes late in a flurry of buggies, bottles and trailing coats, it's too long since you had a baby in your life. I suggest you either get pregnant, or borrow someone else's baby for a bit.

But better early than late

If you have five minutes to spare when you arrive in church you can collect your thoughts, and remind yourself why you are there. You can give your child a hug and if he is old enough to read, seek out the hymns of the day in the hymn book and look at the words. You have a moment to look up the readings for the day. You have a moment to say hello to someone else. You have a moment to pray. You have a moment to take the three-year-old to the loo.

Children in church: do's and don'ts

Any moment of any church service is a teaching opportunity. For example, in Catholic churches a bell is rung at important points in the Mass to remind us that Christ is present. At a wedding I heard the very bright little girl behind me, as the bell was rung, ask her father loudly, 'What does that bell mean?' to which he replied, quick as a flash, 'SHUSH'.

After the service I asked the little girl what she thought the bell meant. 'It means we have to be quiet,' she said, very confidently. 'No, it doesn't,' I said. 'It means Jesus is with us right here.' She gave me a look. Well, wouldn't you? Daddy is always right, when you are three.

So when bringing children to church, try these ideas for making your life easier:

- Don't bring food into church, except baby's milk.
- Don't sit behind a pillar or at the back in the fear that somehow your child's presence has to be hidden away. 'Parents are often cowed into lurking at the back where the children have no hope of seeing or hearing', said a mother of three under-eights.
- Don't bring sick children into church. They will throw up all over the lady in the mink coat in the pew in front. It happened to me: it can happen to you.
- Don't worry about what other people are thinking. You know what stage your child is at: they don't. 'There is tension as regards noise levels, in the parish between older parishioners and families with young children. They don't seem to understand that we don't want to give them a clip around the ear and a good hiding when we get home,' observed a mother of three.

But also think about:

- Remembering that the person whose behaviour your children are most likely to copy in church is YOU. So if you are more occupied with looking around, whispering, checking your watch, fidgeting with your hair, rummaging in your handbag or ticking your child off than with praying or being part of the service, your child will follow suit and will not place any importance on what is going on in the church. Focus genuinely on your own worship, if you want your child to learn to focus on his.
- Sitting behind a family with slightly older children than yours who are relatively tranquil and calm in church ... try it, and watch your children unconsciously imitate them.
- Trying not to get drawn into *sotto voce* discussions about anything and everything. This is your time to pray and you don't need to feel guilty if you deflect a child's attempt at conversation with 'I'm praying now, we'll talk about that after church'. No need to be censorious: the child who sits and

thinks for a while, who lets her mind wander, is using her time in church well because she is allowing it to be a different kind of time. Even if she allows her mind to wander off on a train of thought which ends up with a random remark that has nothing to do with worship (as far as you can see), it does not matter too much: what matters is that the fact of being in church is making her *think*.

- Ignoring your children. There, I said it! As long as they aren't running around, go within to your own prayerful space and tell the little person tugging on your sleeve, 'later'.

- Talking with your smaller children a little beforehand about who they will pray for today. With older children, do them the honour of letting their prayers be private. See if you can check out the readings in advance and chat briefly with them beforehand to get them interested.

- Bringing a plastic, watertight bottle of water. Churches aren't as cool as they are always cracked up to be.

- Frequently replenishing the contents of the God bag with new reading matter or reading-aloud matter. Try browsing www.stpauls.org.uk for activity books.

- Sitting where the child can see the 'action'. Some priests and pastors are better than others at involving children ... but they all know that their future depends on doing so.

- Instead of shushing, scolding or chatting with your bored child, getting him to be aware of what is happening in the service. Explain, occasionally and briefly, what is going on. 'Now the vicar's saying special prayers for everyone. Now we are going to pray for sick people/peace/the church.' The service is for the child as much as for anyone else. He needs to know what's happening and feel involved.

- If you are breastfeeding, go ahead – this is the best baby-soother in the world.

- Relaxing. Above all! Take a deep breath and let it out ... let your shoulders drop, your muscles go limp ... be peaceful. Peacefulness is catching.

- Singing along when you are meant to sing. Get the children to sing and make sure they know the tunes. It will burn up a bit of energy.

- Joining in the prayers, and making sure the children are joining in too. Before you know it they will have several prayers learnt by heart.
- Grabbing any jobs going which children can be part of – collections, offertory, tidying hymn books – and get your children on the team. It will boost your child's self-esteem to feel important and involved, and create a reason for being there which your child can see the point of: 'They NEED me!'
- Making the most of any Sunday school or children's liturgy available. If your child is shy, offer to help out yourself to help your child feel more confident with the group.
- Going to different types of service. You will probably find the bog-standard family service becomes your regular haunt, but children also relish a bit of pomp and circumstance now and again.

And here's a very big DON'T. Don't harbour censorious feelings about other people's children misbehaving in church. You are NOT in church to feel smug. The fact is, every child is on a learning curve and at any one time in a congregation there will be some children who've learned to behave and a lot more children who are just starting out.

Experience, familiarity and steadily growing understanding of what being in church is all about will work their magic on most children in time, but it does take time – and a capacious God bag.

Note

1. 'Work expands so as to fill the time available for its completion', C. Northcote Parkinson, in *The Economist*, 1955. Never truer than at 8.50 on a Sunday morning.

Water and wine

24

I came that they may have life and have it abundantly.

John 10.10

Acts of hospitality have tremendous significance in the life of Christ and his followers, as told in the New Testament. All the way from the welcome extended to Jesus by the family of Lazarus to the precise instructions given to the apostles on the acceptance of hospitality on their travels, hospitality crops up continually and weaves in and out of Jesus' own stories.

Jesus' mission began with an act of hospitality at a wedding; the wedding at Cana was an everyday occasion, on which an everyday disaster struck; a disaster which every host and hostess dreads but which threatens nobody in life or limb. Nobody is going to be seriously hurt but certainly the self-esteem of the host family and especially the bride and groom will be irreparably damaged.

The more one reads the Gospels, the more one feels, on the whole, that it must all have really happened (some atheist writers believe the Gospels are fabricated) because, to borrow a phrase from tabloid journalism, you couldn't make it up. Nobody would decide to invent an unexplained phenomenon like turning water into wine at a wedding. I do not wish to dismiss the theological significance of the miracle. The materials that Jesus worked with formed a perfect bridge between the water of baptism and the wine of the Eucharist, and the wedding is replete with imagery. Yet the theology tends to overlook that this was a real wedding – and wherever there is a wedding, a mother-in-law joke cannot be far away.

If the Gospel writers wanted to invent a miracle that was intended as a sign of Jesus' divinity, surely they would have chosen something a bit more Old Testament – parting the waters of the River Jordan, perhaps? Some impressive pillars of fire and cloud? A thunderbolt? Instead we get a miracle with the production values not of a Hollywood epic but of a TV situation comedy. This was not an Old Testament, Mosaic kind of disaster, but instead a small, domestic disaster. The values of miracle-making have moved from the epic landscape of Charlton Heston playing Moses in *The Ten Commandments* into a neighbourhood more easily inhabited by Dawn French as *The Vicar of Dibley*.

One message of the story of the wedding at Cana is surely that the cares and concerns of ordinary people are not to be dismissed as unimportant. An anxious bridal party's dawning horror as it became gradually clear that their wine supplies were not equal to the task in hand was a real concern. These were real people; they were beloved of God and equal in the eyes of God to the highest in the land.

Another point to the story is that hospitality matters – kindness to strangers is important in Christianity. It is also important in all religions, which does suggest that hospitality is something that does not come easily to us. Religion is the place where human nature tries to better itself, and the common theme of hospitality that joins together our great faiths suggests that in this area we have always needed a lot of encouragement to be friendly, to welcome each other into our homes, to have codes of trust whereby strangers can feel welcome in our homes, and to be generous to guests. It is heartening, for a natural stay-at-home such as me, to realize that since the first civilizations, people have not found it easy to be welcoming and have misunderstood each other's intentions in being so.

Years ago my Latin teacher, a very scholarly Polish woman who had spent all her summers in Greece since the Second World War, told me how angry she felt when Western backpackers arrived for the first time in the Greek islands during the 1960s. She heard young Westerners telling each other tales of the legendary generosity of the islanders, who opened their houses and laid food on their tables to the young newcomers and refused any payment.

'The fact was', fumed my Latin teacher, 'that in the early 1960s the islanders looked at the backpackers arriving off the first holiday ferry boats and saw kids with bare feet, bare legs, dressed in what appeared to be rags. They assumed that since they were dressed so poorly, they must be destitute, and they offered them what help they could. They had no idea, at first, of how much richer these young people were than they were themselves. And the young people exploited that kindness by accepting all the hospitality on offer and paying nothing for it.'

For a short while, she believed, many Greek islanders were victims of their own noble tradition of hospitality, a tradition not designed to cope with the pressures of modern tourism. She believed that this misunderstanding poisoned the attitude of many Greek families to visiting Western travellers for years to come.

Being welcoming, being hospitable, requires some trust and understanding between the giver and the taker. The giver needs to feel he is not being judged and belittled for the poverty of his offerings and the taker needs to feel that he can reciprocate in some way.

Giving hospitality freely, without anxiety and without fear of being snubbed is, paradoxically, more difficult in an affluent society like ours. To consider again the trials of the poor wedding hosts at Cana: how many young couples are there now in the UK who simply do not get married because they do not feel they can afford the kind of lavish do that their friends expect?

As I write, the average cost of a wedding in the UK is nearly £20,000 – and that does not count the obligatory stag and hen parties. (These are Saturnalian evenings or even entire weekends away, when the bride and groom take their closest friends out to celebrate the making of vows of faithfulness – by drinking vodka straight from a bottle.)

British marriage is in a crisis of hospitality inflation. The outer trappings of marriage have outreached themselves to the point where most people cannot afford to contemplate it. The important act of standing up in front of friends and relations declaring eternal fidelity has disappeared from view. In its place we find the problem of whether the bridesmaid's dresses are sexy enough and whether the reception has a 'theme' or not.

And it is not just weddings we have managed to spoil with our escalating expectations. The simple act of having a few friends round for a meal was turned by our ancestors into the terrifying ordeal of the Dinner Party, a ritual of elegance and sparkling conversation between men and women in faultless evening dress, arranged in a neat alternate pattern around a table groaning with impossibly complicated dishes, the finest wines, china and plate. Over the past fifty years the Dinner Party superficially lost some of its archaic trappings – at least we do not have to worry about the order of precedence required by the differing rank of our guests as they walk into the dining room – and turned into a more relaxed affair often eaten in the kitchen. But is it really so relaxed? We transferred our capacity for envy, scene-stealing and one-upmanship away from the capacity to parade silver plate and footmen behind every lady's chair to our own cooking skills, our choice of ingredients ... and our kitchens. In today's affluent homes, more money is spent on the kitchen than on any other room in the house.

Getting married should mean simply standing up in front of one's friends and family and promising publicly, and in front of God, to be true to each other until death. This is what marriage is about, not flowers, dresses and getting the best band to play. Inviting friends into one's home should be about friendship, not showing off black-marble work surfaces. In your home, your friends should feel welcome, not cowed.

The concept of the 'church social' may not make the heart exactly race with excitement, but when we look at the solitary, private existences most people lead, is it really such a bad idea to draw single people into a loose but loving network of families?

Let me introduce you to Fr Peter McGrath. Everyone in the 100,000-strong Family Groups movement in Australia knows this energetic, rubicund 67-year-old, pugnacious to the point of brusque and bouncy to the point of overwhelming. Inspired partly by his own experiences of recovery from alcoholism through Alcoholics Anonymous (an organization whose Christian roots are discreetly veiled nowadays), Fr Peter has pioneered the idea of drawing members of a church congregation closer together by means of Family Groups.

These are more or less randomly allocated 'subsets' of the congregation, circles of households who pledge to meet up regularly, to take a supportive interest in each other's lives and generally to re-create the friendly village mentality which we all think we have lost and which we probably never had very much of anyway.

A typical Family Group of the type McGrath (he hates being called 'Father' – which strikes me as rather a handicap for a man called by God to become a Catholic priest) has founded, comprises eight to ten households but may easily be started off by far fewer than this. McGrath has a speaking circuit of churches in Australia to promote the concept and has a characteristic opening gambit: 'I talk at first all about loving one another and all that. And then I say, "You don't realize it but the people in the pew right behind you are just so ugly."'

Instantly the entire congregation will half turn their heads out of automatic curiosity. McGrath's little spiel continues: 'Now hands up if you didn't know the names of the people behind you!' Invariably a substantial forest of hands goes up.

Far too many people, McGrath points out, go to church and see the same faces every week without knowing their names. The simple courtesy of knowing someone's name is constantly shirked and avoided, and the more familiar a face becomes, the more inhibited we feel about saying, 'Look, I am sorry, I see you every Sunday, but what is your name?'

How many people do you see every day whose names you do not know? How many of them would be able to put a name to your face? If you work in a town, the answer will be in the dozens. You walk past the same man selling newspapers, the same security guard on the door, the same bored young woman at the reception desk every day. I buy my stamps from the same man in the post office year in and year out and I have never had the courage to say, as I take my change, 'By the way, what's your name?'

It is strange that in a faith where names are so important, cemented into the baptism rite itself, that we shy away from finding each other's out. A 'name badge Sunday' is quite a good ice-breaking way out of the embarrassment of not knowing someone's name even though you know their face.

The initial inspiration for Family Groups should come from the church itself – either the priest/pastor acting alone or the parish council. A Family Group is not a very formal arrangement. It may have been assembled by the parish council, but it should not look like a parish council – no chair, vice-chair, treasurer or minutes, but more like a family party. The group may include families from different churches in an ecumenical grouping – it is in fact an excellent way of reaching across into other branches of the Christian family in your district, and also of reaching the non-churchgoers in households where some go to church and others do not.

Try grouping together families who are not already friends or acquaintances and mixing up ages and stages – a young couple, an older couple with teenagers, a single or two or three. As long as there is one family, couple or single-with-spare-time who agree firmly to be the organizers of the group – say for a year initially, then on a rotating basis with others – then you've got the core of something big.

Invite families to join, and get their active agreement to attend a function. Give them plenty of notice, ring and remind several weeks before and the week before as well. Never, never be tempted to change the date because it clashes with something ... that way madness lies.

The first function should be very simple, low cost and preferably on a pot-luck, bring-a-bottle basis. Competitive entertaining needs to be discouraged at the outset, otherwise less confident or well-off members of the group will feel very uncomfortable when their time comes round to be host. Have a time limit and make it short so that everyone is sent home enjoying themselves (same principle as children's parties). Remember the point is to get members of the group to mix and talk to each other, in the hope of forming new connections, not for the two main families involved to sit in a huddle together and moan about their children's unsatisfactory schoolteacher. Start a diary of birthdays, wedding anniversaries and other special events in members' lives.

Most importantly, the Family Group offers an opportunity for treating each other exactly as you would treat Christ if he came to your house. Having said that, take into account the reluctance of most people to get involved in anything remotely church-y ... and be prepared for the first meeting to seem rather a damp squib.

And here's the difference between the kind of hospitality Jesus looks for from us and the kind we usually indulge in. Most people are looking for a specific result from their social encounters, a result that benefits themselves: a bit of targeted networking, a deal pushed forward, a new sexual encounter, or just the chance to get drunk. Most of the time we get together people for our *own* purposes, not to offer friendship to *them*. The elaborate wedding ceremonies of our day are for the glory and pride of the bride and groom and their families; they are not intended to strengthen the wedding vows by the guests.

Turn the usual way of seeing social occasions on its head: try doing it not for yourself but for others. Paradoxically, we lift a great burden from our shoulders once we learn to accept the course of events.

'Whoever comes are the right people and the only people who are meant to come, whether it's one person or a hundred,' says Fr McGrath. 'Whatever happens was the right thing to happen and was the only thing that could happen. You have done your best in preparing. Place the whole gathering in God's hands.'

'Place the whole gathering in God's hands . . .' – not bad advice to anyone giving a party.

Salt

25

> You are salt for the earth. But if salt loses its taste, what can make it salty again? It is good for nothing, and can only be thrown out to be trampled under people's feet.
>
> *Matthew 5.13*

Christ told us we must be the Salt and Light of the world. We've talked about light quite a bit so far, but what about salt? Why do Christ's followers have to be salty?

In Christ's day, salt was used to preserve food and to flavour it. Nobody knew about it being bad for your heart in those days, so salt was regarded as a thoroughly good thing. There are several folk tales and fairy stories, similar to the story of King Lear which we know through Shakespeare's play, about a king (or a rich man) who asks his favourite daughter how much she loves him.

She says 'I love you as fresh meat loves salt.' The king is outraged by the inelegance of her reply – which seems to be a fairy story version of 'I need you like a fish needs a bicycle', since fresh meat is by definition unsalted.

At the end of the story, in some versions after the daughter has been banished, met with perils and finally reunited with her now broken father, she prepares him a meal without salt ... and of course it tastes perfectly horrible, and so the father realizes that meat needs salt. The father is always foolish in the story, and there is often a hint that the love he demands from his daughter or daughters is incestuous. Fairy stories are not always sweet.

Salt is no ordinary flavouring – it is at once seductive and repellent. It makes you want more and less of it at the same time. It acts as a preservative. Salt is an abrasive, gritty stuff which when rubbed into wounds hurts hideously. It corrodes and tarnishes and leaves its mark, for all its innocent white crystalline appearance.

And salt, of course, has a remarkable physical similarity to sugar, a similarity exploited by anyone who has indulged in the ancient communal-dining-room joke of swapping the two over. Now they didn't have sugar in Jesus' time . . . they had honey to sweeten things. Jesus did not ask us to be honey and light – sweetness and light – but *salt* and light.

Christians today are not very welcome. Politicians are allowed to be seen going to church as a kind of badge of propriety, but let them once suggest that they pray at home, or that they allow their faith to guide their decisions, and they become reviled as monsters of delusion. Some professions, from teachers to airline staff, are requested to hide any signs of Christianity for fear of offending those of other faiths.

Britain's Prime Minister, Gordon Brown, was considered to be sailing close to the wind when he dared quote the Bible in his first prime ministerial speech to his political party: even though he took care not to mention Jesus by name, but only cited His words 'Suffer the little children to come unto Me' as a vaguely identified 'biblical saying' – for all the world as though Jesus Christ were an anonymous writer of greetings card mottos.

Christians are noticed only when their churches swell their numbers and their coffers with brash commercial appeals to the desperation of the poor and uneducated; or when they are closing down their churches and selling off the buildings for want of support. Christians are disliked for either being too salty – saying things people do not want to hear, mainly about morality and sin, or else for being too sugary – trying to coat the pill of real life with a dreamy belief that one day in the afterlife everything will get better.

Being 'trampled under people's feet' is rather what it feels like to be a Christian in the secular West. So maybe we lost our flavour somewhere?

Salt, as opposed to sugar, is a little akin to that mysterious commodity everybody wants in society, an 'ethos'. Parents who never darken the doors of a church often seek out church schools for their children, or schools with a religious foundation, because they like the idea of the 'ethos' in the school. They don't really care very much where that ethos has come from, as long as it's an 'ethos'.

Yet the truth is that the 'ethos' they like has come directly from the Christian faith – and from nowhere else. Our role in the world is as its salt – *not* as its sugar. There is a difference between the desire to sweeten and sugar-coat the world, to sprinkle it with sentimentality in order to render it easier to swallow, and the injunction to be salt to the world, not masking its flavour but bringing it out – bringing out its meaning and underlying truth.

Faith seems to be used as a sugar-coating in a lot of Christian discourse, and it is a shame. Any quick dip into the world of Christian publishing in the USA will reveal hundreds of self-help manuals which have been written to present the 'Christian' way of doing this or that – the Christian way to get out of debt, the Christian way to win a good job, the Christian way to lose weight; books that address the problems of affluent Westerners and try to put a Christian slant on them.

The Christian weight-loss movement, for example, began in the 1950s with a book entitled *Pray Your Weight Away*, written by a Presbyterian minister with the wonderfully appropriate name of Charlie Shedd. As America got fatter, so did the Christian weight-loss business, as seen in popular slim-and-pray programmes such as the 'Weigh Down' workshops across America, marrying that nation's fondness for obsessing about its weight to its taste for cheerful, upbeat evangelism.

There is something about such books and programmes that smacks of the 'false prophets' of whom the Apostle John speaks: 'Those false prophets speak about matters of the world, and the world listens to them because they *belong to the world*.' 'What would Jesus eat?' asks the title of one Christian weight-loss programme. Such a question is so much 'of this world' that it cannot be aligned with anything Jesus ever talked about. When so many do not have enough to eat or clean water to drink, decent accommodation or a life free from fear of oppression and war, then fretting over whether Jesus would order the steak and chips or the chicken salad is patently absurd.

In 2006 a new 'How To' book hit the headlines, and, for once, the usual claim that it had 'taken America by storm' seemed almost credible. Under the portentous title *The Secret*, this one really was a biggie because it did not just show you how to achieve small, fiddly, specific goals like marrying the right person or living until 100, but also claimed to show you how to manipulate the entire universe, no less, and to get it to send you all the riches you desire.

The author, a former daytime TV producer called Rhonda Byrne, claims to show readers how to obtain anything they want – anything! Anything at all! By the 'law of attraction', just by thinking about what you are searching for – a rich husband or a parking space, for example – the universe will deliver it to you.

The law of attraction does not really exist. It is a concept based loosely on a metaphor used by hypnotherapy practitioners which describes the phenomenon whereby if we visualize a desired outcome we make it easier for ourselves to achieve it. Hypnotherapists are sometimes reminded that the various metaphors used to describe how our minds work – our use of terms such as the 'subconscious', for example – are only metaphors, not physiological descriptions to be taken literally.

If there is no parking space in a street, no amount of hard concentration will make one appear. Driving into another street might reveal one to you, in which case you need some positive thinking and determination; but you can do this with or without the aid of the universe. The close parallel between *The Secret* and the promises of prayer is a troubling one for a Christian. A quick reading of Byrne seems to echo Christ's words, 'Ask and it shall be given'; it is just too close for comfort. Go through the book and cross out the word 'Universe', and replace it with 'God', and what do you get? A kind of handbook on prayer? Is this all that prayer amounts to – just giving God a shopping list?

No – because *The Secret* is the idea that the 'universe' basically revolves around YOU, yes, you personally, the reader of *The Secret*. Rhonda Byrne proclaims: 'The Universe is supporting me in everything I do. The universe meets all my needs immediately.'

It is an utterly self-obsessed creed. Byrne's list of things for which we can 'ask' the universe, in the certain hope of receiving, is composed entirely of material goods – things of this world straight from the pages of a blockbuster sex-and-shopping novel: abundant wealth, big swanky houses, well-paid jobs and advantageous marriages to rich and beautiful spouses.

A baby assumes that he is the centre of the universe; one sign of increased cognitive awareness is the discovery that one is not the centre of the universe. Rhonda Byrne's adherents are being told to go back to infancy. It is the ultimate example of turning the Christian promise to be 'salt and light' to the world into an infantile desire to have everything coated in sugar so that everything tastes nice.

By contrast, what our faith tells us about prayer is quite the opposite. In prayer we lose ourselves; we offer ourselves up and we submit ourselves to God's will, rather than sending Him off with a list of requests. We say, 'Your Will be done', not 'my will be done'. We look at what we have and we are glad of it, and use it well, rather than wishing and longing for the wealth and riches promised in *The Secret*.

The book claims a 'biblical' basis and Mark 4.25 is quoted to support it: 'Those who have something will be given more, and those who have nothing will have taken away from them even the little they have.'

Taking single verses out of the Gospels as though they were sound bites from a politician's speech is dishonest. This verse is set into Jesus' discourse about the parable of the sower. The verses before it run as follows: 'Jesus continued: "Does anyone ever bring in a lamp and put it under a bowl or under the bed? Doesn't he put it on the lampstand? Whatever is hidden away will be brought out into the open, and whatever is covered up will be uncovered. Listen then, if you have ears!" He also said to them: "Pay attention to what you hear! The same rules you use to judge others will be used by God to judge you – but with even greater severity."'

This is a mystical passage in which Jesus talks of the difference between those who use what God has given them, and those who do not; between those who judge others harshly, and those who do not. There are many arguments about what it means ... but it definitely is not about finding a parking space on a busy shopping afternoon, or about material wealth.

Any good psychologist will tell you that if you fall into habits of negative thinking, then you will damage your confidence, make yourself over-anxious and thereby injure your success in any undertaking. Any good psychologist will advise you to go into a new venture believing you can and will succeed. Thus far *The Secret* is harmless and benign.

But *The Secret*, and many newly coined spiritualities, goes further than this. It maintains that all religions are essentially the same, composed of the same spiritual essence or whatever . . . the same sugary mixture coating them all, if you like.

G. K. Chesterton, the Catholic novelist and essayist of the early twentieth century, observed in one of his characteristic paradoxes that it was commonplace to remark on how all religions look different on the outside, yet are basically the same at root. Yet, pointed out Chesterton, the opposite is really true: because all religions have rather similar appearances, with priestly groups, ceremonies, buildings of worship, monastic traditions and rites of passage often having superficial similarities. It is only, he added, when you scratch the surface that you find how very different they are.

Sugar-coated spirituality only leads us away from the truth, which is that sometimes our faith is a little bit salty, a little bit gritty and hard to swallow. It is not necessarily God's will that you get the biggest car on the block; it is not for us to tell God precisely how to answer our prayers.

The well-informed Christian parent can afford to be bold in arguing with proponents of other spiritualities, especially ones which are blatantly full of hokum. And most importantly, besides being a little salty and awkward, we don't forget that the other side of the picture of our relationship with the world is as a light: 'so that, *seeing your good works*, they may give praise to your Father in heaven'.

A sword

Let nothing disturb thee,
Nothing affright thee
All things are passing;
God never changeth;
Patient endurance
Attaineth to all things;
Who God possesseth
In nothing is wanting;
Alone God sufficeth.

Words written in St Teresa of Avila's
breviary (1515 to 1582) known as 'St Teresa's bookmark'

Blessed are you when people abuse you and persecute you and speak all kinds of calumny against you falsely on my account. Rejoice and be glad, for your reward will be great in heaven; this is how they persecuted the prophets before you.

Matthew 5.11–12

Let faith be my shield, and let hope be my steed
'Gainst the dragons of anger, the ogres of greed
And let me set free with the sword of my youth
From the castle of darkness the power of the truth.

from a hymn written by Jan Struther, 1901–53,
Songs of Praise *(OUP)*

This is a toolkit containing some unwieldy objects; hedges, alarm clocks, wine, biscuit barrels. Some of these tools are useful in keeping your relationship with your child in good shape, some are for fixing family life and others are for dealing with the community at large, a community which is increasingly wary of anyone claiming to belong to a religion.

We have looked at the need to be aware and awake, to be still and contemplative, to be faithful and hopeful. We have considered the need to let people judge our faith by our works; the need sometimes to put on the right face for the occasion in the hope it becomes the true face; and the need to allow our children to turn out as they will, cherishing and making the best of talent but also avoiding squeezing them into any agenda we have set for them in advance.

The Christian family home is a holy place simply because of the love that exists there, not because of rituals or prohibitions within its walls. Living family life according to the words of Jesus may mean trying to live a bit more simply, or it may mean living with a more open hand. It may mean setting boundaries but most of all it should mean enjoying the lasting things of life – story, companionship, kindness, the beauties of nature.

And we have looked at how supportive and strengthening an active faith community can be for families of all ages and stages, shapes and sizes, and how it can help us to look sceptically at any movement that promises us incredible benefits.

The most important 'tool' in the kit, of course, is Love, but there is another which is used throughout and is much in need today.

One of the most frequently used words in the book of Acts, the stories about what happened after Jesus' resurrection, is the Greek word *parrhesia*, meaning cheerful boldness in the face of danger and opposition. 'Be not afraid' or 'fear not' are words that echo constantly throughout the Gospels (and that were chosen as the motto of his papacy by Pope John Paul II).

There cannot have been since those times a more difficult time in Western Europe to own up to being a Christian, especially to own up to raising one's children as Christians. This sounds like an extravagant claim. Christians can hardly claim to be persecuted in the UK, and they seem – or certain sects of them seem – to be very much in the ascendant in the USA.

The picture is different elsewhere in the world. Some aid workers estimate that Christians are persecuted in some 60 different countries. According to the charities Open Doors and Aid to the Church in Need, up to 230 million Christians are suffering for their faith in various ways ranging from denial of legal property rights, eviction, employment discrimination to intimidation, imprisonment, torture and murder.

Here in the UK, Christians can walk the streets safely and have our own schools. We can worship freely. We even have an 'established' Church; Christians sit in Parliament, in the House of Lords, solely to represent their Church.

There is no doubt that Christianity is the dominant creed and a powerful shaper of society's values. However, over recent years a subtle sea-change has taken place. The popularity of fanatically atheist writers such as Professor Richard Dawkins, Oxford Professor for the Public Understanding of Science, and the influential children's author Philip Pullman, has brought into being a highly aggressive new movement against religion in general. This is a movement that does more than disdain religion: this movement really wants religion stamped out. This movement has no qualms about proselytizing: a free copy of Dawkins' book, *The God Delusion*, was sent to all Labour MPs in time for Parliament's summer break in 2007. Christianity is probably the easiest, safest, most fashionable target in the world for anyone to attack. Attacking Christianity requires absolutely no courage at all. It is a big target – you can hardly miss it. Many terrible things have been done by people in Christ's name; Christianity is visible; and it is old, providing a rich heritage of mistakes. It is a very safe target, because its basic tenet of 'turning the other cheek' means that the attacker can be certain that he will not be subject to any kind of revenge or *fatwa*. It is the most fashionable target to attack because its extraordinary success has made it part of the Establishment, and nothing looks more fashionable than appearing to attack the Establishment.

Christians can still walk the streets safely. Or can we? And Christians can have their own schools – but will they for much longer? Successive attempts to curtail the provision of specifically Christian schools within the state sector have been made, and will continue to be made. There is a strong feeling in Westminster that religious schools are a bad thing in general and that church schools are a problem, not a solution. Forty years ago being a Christian required no courage to speak of because it was the 'default option'.

Now it requires real courage, especially for a young person, to admit to faith. St Peter's blunder on the night of the Crucifixion, denying that he knew Christ, becomes increasingly an attractive option.

The tradition of protest among the young has a glow of courage about it – but how much courage does it take for a student to join a fashionable cause such as protesting against global warming? Virtually none, because it is the cool thing to do. How much courage does it take, on the other hand, for a student to affirm Christian faith?

The first words the angel spoke to Mary when bringing her the news that she would bear Jesus were 'Fear not' (Luke 10), and 'fear not' is among Jesus' most common phrases in the Gospels, echoed again on Easter Sunday by the angel who greets the women coming to Jesus' tomb.

There is not a single shred of evil committed in Christ's name that cannot be laid at the door of failure to hear the message clearly and to live it out honestly. The faith Christ bequeathed to us works if you put it into practice properly ... but if you twist it, horror results. A child beaten by someone in the name of Christianity is beaten by a misguided human being who has severely misunderstood his or her own faith; a murder committed in God's name is committed by an even more misguided human being, and a war in Christ's name is waged using Christ as an excuse.

As Kate McCann, the mother of the child whose disappearance on holiday in Portugal in 2007 gripped the British public's imagination, has said, it is not God who does terrible things, but human beings. And as her husband Gerry has said, the community of faith surrounding the wronged parents is what gives them courage to go on with life and caring for their surviving children.

'A robin redbreast in a cage puts all Heaven in a rage', wrote William Blake, the English poet whose essential Christianity and belief in God is skimmed over when he is described as a 'visionary' or a 'mystic'. If we do not have the courage to challenge the greater affronts to Heaven, we can at least act out our faith by working against the smaller injustices nearer home: standing up for a bullied colleague, supporting a school fighting against violence, helping in a homeless shelter. We can let our faith be known through smaller good works in the hope that we can build up courage for larger ones.

The time for *parrhesia* is clearly come again – and this virtue is akin to the 'sword of my youth' in the hymn quoted above. It is not anger – or arrogance – or aggression – but a *cheerful* boldness, accompanied by good humour. The only way to silence critics is by acting out our faith in our own lives, and doing so with cheerful courage.

> In love there is no room for fear,
> but perfect love drives out fear,
> because fear implies punishment
> and whoever is afraid has not come to perfection in love.
> Let us love, then,
> because he first loved us.
>
> *I John 4.18*